ONE WEEK LO▲

▮ ▮PEC▮IVES ON ▮AM▮▮Y LAW

Feminist Perspectives on Family Law assesses the impact that feminism has had upon family law. In addition to issues of longstanding concern for feminists, it examines issues of current legal and political concern, such as civil partnerships, home-sharing, reproductive technologies, and new initiatives in regulating the family through criminal law, including domestic violence and youth justice. Deliberately broad in scope, it takes the view that family law cannot be defined in a traditional way.

Alison Diduck is based in the Faculty of Laws, UCL.

Katherine O'Donovan was formerly at the Department of Law, Queen Mary, University of London.

FEMINIST PERSPECTIVES ON FAMILY LAW

Edited by
Alison Diduck
and
Katherine O'Donovan

Routledge·Cavendish
Taylor & Francis Group
a GlassHouse book

First published 2006 by Routledge-Cavendish
2 Park Square, Milton Park, Abingdon, Oxon OX14 4RN

Simultaneously published in the USA and Canada
by Routledge
270 Madison Avenue, New York, NY 10016

A Glasshouse book

Routledge-Cavendish is an imprint of the Taylor & Francis Group, an informa business

© 2006 Alison Diduck and Katherine O'Donovan

Typeset in Sabon by RefineCatch Limited, Bungay, Suffolk
Printed and bound in Great Britain by Antony Rowe, Chippenham, Wilts

British Library Cataloguing in Publication Data
A catalogue record for this book is available from the British Library

Library of Congress Cataloging in Publication Data
Feminist perspectives on family law / edited by Alison Diduck and Katherine O' Donovan.
p. cm.
ISBN 1–904385–42–7 (hardback) – ISBN 0–415–42036–9 (pbk.) 1. Domestic relations.
2. Women – Legal status, laws, etc. 3. Family violence. 4. Parenting. 5. Feminist theory.
I. Diduck, Alison. II. O'Donovan, Katherine.
K670.F46 2006
346.01'5 – dc22
2006021952

ISBN 10: 1–904385–42–7 (hbk)
ISBN 10: 0–415–42036–9 (pbk)

ISBN 13: 978–1–904385–42–4 (hbk)
ISBN 13: 978–0–415–42036–5 (pbk)

List of Contributors

Anne Bottomley is Senior Lecturer in Law at the University of Kent.

Richard Collier is Professor of Law at Newcastle University.

Alison Diduck is Reader in Law at University College London.

Emily Jackson is Professor of Law at Queen Mary, University of London.

Caroline Jones is Lecturer in Law at the University of Southampton.

Felicity Kaganas is Reader in Law at Brunel University.

Maleiha Malik is Senior Lecturer in Law at King's College London.

Jill Marshall is Lecturer in Law at Queen Mary, University of London.

Ann Mumford is Lecturer in Law at the London School of Economics.

Katherine O'Donovan was formerly Professor of Law at Queen Mary, University of London.

Christine Piper is Professor of Law at Brunel University.

Carol Smart is Professor of Sociology at Manchester University.

Carl Stychin is Professor of Law at the University of Reading.

Simone Wong is Senior Lecturer in Law at the University of Kent.

Acknowledgments |

As teachers of family law who are engaged with feminist and gender issues, we are delighted to present this collection of papers in the Routledge-Cavendish series on Feminist Perspectives. We wish to thank Sally Sheldon, Anne Bottomley and Beverley Brown for inviting us to edit a collection. We are very grateful to Lara Kretzer, tutor and research student at Queen Mary, for her help in sorting out references and style.

Most of the chapters in this volume were presented as papers in July 2004 at a one-day workshop at University College London. We thank Lisa Penfold for her help in organising the day. Routledge-Cavendish, Queen Mary and University College provided funding for the workshop and we are grateful to them. Above all, we thank the contributors to this collection for their enthusiastic engagement with the project and for the stimulating papers they have written.

Alison Diduck and Katherine O'Donovan
December 2005

Contents |

Table of Cases |

Chapter 1
Feminism and Families: *Plus Ça Change?*
Alison Diduck and Katherine O'Donovan

Introduction

While feminist perspectives on all areas of life and law are crucial to achieve a just, nuanced and comprehensive understanding of them, some might think that the family and family law are the first, or at least most obvious, places to start. After all, feminism is concerned to ask questions about the lives of women, and the lives of women have traditionally centred upon their families. In fact, feminist perspectives have been offered upon family relations since a recognised feminist movement began centuries ago. From these, its 'first waves', the feminist movement was concerned, among other things, to secure not only women's political equality with men, but also women's (special) rights to custody of their children; the second wave's campaigns in the mid-twentieth century to promote women's financial self-sufficiency and independence from men also aimed to reveal an ideology of the family that inhibited that goal. Family relations and family law have thus always been as important to women, and therefore to feminism, as have claims to civil, political or legal rights. And importantly, in always asking the 'woman question' and thus rendering both visible and valuable the concerns of women in law, feminist legal theory has also been able to link family law and family relations to women's abilities to make those claims.

Of course, family relations and family law have always been important to men and children also and to their political status, economic activity and claims to citizenship and rights, and it is a feminist perspective that has made this link explicit. The importance of feminist perspectives on family law, therefore, is to bring to light the ways in which the legal regulation of private, *family* relations are also about the regulation of *social and political* relations; they are about the nature and value of dependence and independence, about the balance of social and economic power and about the part that law plays in this regulation. A feminist perspective emphasises the personal as political, and, born as it was of feminist activism, feminist theory is also about the possibility of the transformation or reconstruction of both.

The contributions to this collection about family law are thus feminist in orientation or character not because they necessarily agree about the advantages or disadvantages of, or the causes of or solutions to, gendered living, but because they explore the ways in which law is implicated in that living. And they adopt a range of feminist methodologies to do so. Method, as Maleiha Malik[1] points out, is critical. Feminist methods are about critique: they aim to disrupt; to question; to render problematic the 'objective', the 'neutral' and the 'normal'. Feminist perspectives challenge not only law's claims to objectivity and liberalism's foundational

---

1 Chapter 11.

claims of autonomy[2] and equality,[3] but also legal and social norms[4] and the forms of reasoning that sustain them.[5] Like other feminist work, there is a breadth to the writings here. Some of the chapters draw on traditional legal sources such as cases and statutes; others look to government position papers and parliamentary discussion; yet others are based on interview material and the internet. Contributors adopt conceptual feminist methods,[6] hermeneutic methods,[7] queer theory,[8] discourse analysis,[9] empirical analysis,[10] critique,[11] futurology[12] and social policy analysis.[13] Sometimes they discover that law is amenable to feminist disruption and critique, but often they uncover its resistance and the difficulties that resistance creates in the day-to-day family lives – the family practices[14] – of individual men, women and children.[15]

The perspectives offered in this book can also be called feminist because they address one or more of the themes that many scholars of family law have identified as currently important in transforming the lived reality or material effects of gendered family living.[16] The changing landscapes of family, of feminism and of law mean that the concerns of the twenty-first century are different from those of other times, as are the conceptual and practical tools with which we can engage with them. In the 1970s, campaigns for 'wages for housework', questions like 'why be a wife?', or references to 'the rapist who pays the rent' generated a long moment of challenge to gendered conceptions of family, self and society. Although this challenge was initially directed at perceived male dominance and at the silence and invisibility of women, both sexes came under scrutiny, which led to analyses of dominant and accepted norms in family and personal life.

Different concerns dominated the 1980s. A form of 'pro-family' feminism came to celebrate gender differentiation, including women's roles as mothers. Elements of this pro-familialism remain today, with the expression by some women of a 'you can't have it all' philosophy once they become mothers. Indeed, there is something almost unfashionable for many young women today about the claims their mothers made, and it is feminism that is often blamed for creating unreal

---

2 See, for example, Malik, Chapter 11; O'Donovan and Marshall, Chapter 6.
3 Lacey (1998); in this volume see Smart, Chapter 7; Stychin, Chapter 2; Kaganas, Chapter 8; Piper, Chapter 9; Mumford, Chapter 10.
4 See Stychin, Chapter 2; Jackson, Chapter 4; Bottomley and Wong, Chapter 3.
5 See Jackson, Chapter 4.
6 O'Donovan and Marshall, Chapter 6; Bottomley and Wong, Chapter 3; Jones, Chapter 5.
7 Malik, Chapter 11.
8 Stychin, Chapter 2.
9 Smart, Chapter 7; Kaganas, Chapter 8; Piper, Chapter 9.
10 Piper, Chapter 9; Jones, Chapter 5; Smart, Chapter 7.
11 Collier, Chapter 12.
12 Jackson, Chapter 4.
13 Mumford, Chapter 10; Piper, Chapter 9; Stychin, Chapter 2.
14 Morgan (1996).
15 See, eg, Piper, Chapter 9; Jones, Chapter 5.
16 Collier, Chapter 12; and see Boyd and Young (2004).

expectations for women who try to live their family lives differently, perhaps by 'having it all' and combining paid work with family work.[17]

In contemporary times, questions of labour and political economy and 'who does care and caring?' remain as material as they were twenty or even forty years ago, but feminist theory has also raised new questions. Focus is now also on the ways in which both concepts and material realities are constructed or given meaning, so that previously taken-for-granted concepts like autonomy, rationality, justice, or sex/gender can themselves be unsettled.

Feminist engagements with law and policy have also undergone a form of self-reflection or self-interrogation. While nineteenth- and early twentieth-century feminists relied firmly on the authority of law to effect social and political change, formal law's centrality in maintaining the gender order seems no longer to be so clear.[18] To modern feminists, law is still important, but even it must be redefined, and it must be analysed in terms of the part it plays in conjunction with other regimes or 'discourses' to regulate our familial and gendered lives.

As a result of the work of feminists in all of these times we have been able to bring to light not only inequalities at the material and symbolic levels of the private, but also their spillover effects into politics, paid work and public life in general; the terms of the debates in politics, in fiscal and social policy and in the labour movement have shifted accordingly. We *can* now ask, for example, if it is the structure of the labour market or, as Ann Mumford[19] suggests, the tax and benefit system, rather than the individual choices of women, which means they 'can't have it all', and we can also ask how we contribute in our day-to-day performance of gender to its material effects.[20] This shift, we argue, this legitimation of previously unvoiced and unvoiceable concerns and observations, can be counted as another of feminism's success stories in the family law field.[21]

We have also become able to redraw the boundaries around *ways of thinking about* ourselves and the ways we live. Contributors here, for example, illustrate the importance of entirely new ways of thinking about intimate and affective connections in their proposal for a new paradigm from which questions can be posed about relationships of care and support.[22] Even apart from the question of why the dyadic relationship is privileged over others, Anne Bottomley and Simone Wong[23] and Carl Stychin[24] ask: 'When does a couple become a shared household and when does a shared household become a couple?' For our purposes, we could also ask 'when do they each become a "family?" ' and, for this question, we could also draw upon Caroline Jones's[25] and Emily Jackson's[26] challenging of the

---

17 Douglas and Michaels (2004).
18 See, eg, Smart (1989).
19 Chapter 10.
20 See, eg, Collier, Chapter 12.
21 Philipps (2004).
22 Chapter 3.
23 Chapter 3.
24 Chapter 2.
25 Chapter 5.
26 Chapter 4.

'naturalness' of parenthood. In the twenty-first century, the meaning, value and *politics* of terms such as 'couple', 'parent' and 'family' lend themselves to feminist scrutiny and challenge.

The terms of the legal debates have also shifted, and it is certainly important to note that we now have a woman Law Lord: Baroness Hale's contribution to ideas of equality and justice in family living has been considerable.[27] Even before her appointment, however, judicial statements such as those in *Gillick v West Norfolk and Wisbech Area Health Authority*,[28] *R v R*,[29] or *White v White*[30] dramatically changed the discourse around legal obligations, roles and responsibilities in intimate living. While serious difficulties remain with many of these decisions, and while legal change certainly cannot be a guarantee of behavioural or attitudinal change, it would be puerile, if not irresponsible, to suggest that these cases have not opened up a space for a feminist reconsideration of family living.

Feminist challenges have also had an impact upon legislation. While much remains problematic about the ways in which it is interpreted and implemented, as Felicity Kaganas notes,[31] Part IV of the Family Law Act 1996 clearly reveals a feminist influence. Further, although there are other difficulties about the way they are framed and experienced, provisions for maternity, paternity, adoption and parenting leave arguably also owe their credibility to a feminist influence in creating a space in which conversations about them could be held. But although family law has sometimes responded to feminist challenges, as we shall see, sometimes it has not. Consider, for example, the fact that only one half of female pensioners are entitled to a full basic state pension, compared with 90 per cent of men, and that of these, approximately only one third receive the pension as a result of their own contributions; the remainder rely upon entitlement through their husbands' contributions. Only 30 per cent of women have an additional private pension provision, compared with over 70 per cent of men.[32] And so, while women have the same ability formally to accrue retirement pensions as men, because their patterns of work differ markedly from the 40-year full-time model on which pension accrual and entitlement are based, women, disproportionately to men, tend to face the real possibility of poverty on retirement. It is not by chance, recognised the Minister of State for Pensions, that two-thirds of those benefiting from Pension Credit (the means-tested top-up to state pension provision) are women.[33]

At other times, the legal response to the feminist challenge has taken the

---

27 See, for example, *Ghaidan v Mendoza* [2004] UKHL 30; *R (on the application of Williamson) v Secretary of State for Education and Employment* [2005] UKHL 15; *Miller v Miller; McFarlane v McFarlane* [2006] UKHL 24.

28 [1986] AC 112.

29 [1991] 4 All ER 481.

30 [2001] AC 596.

31 Chapter 8.

32 Wicks, The Rt Hon Malcolm, MP, Minister of State for Pensions (2004), Speech to TUC Conference, 'Women and Pensions'.

33 *Ibid.*

form of a type of backlash, similar to the formal equality backlash that was part of the 1984 amendments to the Matrimonial Causes Act 1973,[34] while at still other times, the gulf between symbolic legal statements and behavioural change remains vast. In other words, whether there has been a fundamental re-ordering of family living both inside and outside the home remains open to question. As Richard Collier[35] says, men and women do not come to law or to their families as fixed, gendered subjects; rather, the meaning and effects of gender are created, constructed or shaped by what we do. Both law and family living are gendering processes that have profound material consequences for men, women and children.

The gendering effects of family living are difficult to disentangle from law, but are as complicit as law in claims to and ideas of justice. Susan Okin observed in 1989 that the family 'is not conducive to the rearing of citizens with a strong sense of justice'.[36] Looking at gender-related role allocations in a family through the eyes of children growing up therein leads to interesting perspectives. Okin argued that injustice resulting from the division of labour between the sexes destroys 'the family's potential to be the crucial first school where children develop a sense of fairness'.[37] Okin's themes are familiar from feminist work of the past forty years: the division of household and paid labour by sex; the gendered practices of family life; unequal pay in paid work; and assumptions about workers as free individualists. Given developmental theory on the identification of children with the parent of the same sex and the assignation of primary parenting within the existing gender structure, it is not surprising to find mothering reproduced in girls.[38] But although girl-children may see a model in their mothers, they may also be aware of power and inequalities. For all children, a perception of inequalities of power and resources in their families may be an education in injustice.

How far have we come from Okin's powerful observations? Collier's[39] concerns with materialist and power aspects of gender relations and his implied criticism of neglect of these in recent feminist work challenge us to reflect upon this question. Whereas Okin's vision of a genderless society seems as far away today as it was at the time of her writing, her emphasis on the material conditions of the conventional division of labour between the sexes remains pertinent today, notwithstanding its expression in the new discourse of individual choice. Conventional gender performances still exert a pull once a woman becomes a wife and mother, and this pressure may come as much from within, with love and dreams for their children taking precedence over other work roles. Too often, however, this is represented as 'choice', whereas what lie beneath are power differentials and conventional gendered assumptions. As Bren Neale and Carol Smart wrote in 2002, the identities of mothers tend to be bound up primarily with their children

---

34 Smart (1984).
35 Chapter 12; and (2001).
36 Okin (1989), p 170.
37 *Ibid*, vii.
38 Chodorow (1978).
39 Chapter 12.

while fathers' identities tend to be bound up primarily with their employment.[40] Placing these findings within the rhetoric of 'choice' simply masks this, the normalising power of gender and family roles. Neale and Smart conclude that 'a strong element of choice is still associated with a mother's decision to enter or stay in the labour market, and the same element of choice is still associated with a father's decision to care'.[41]

For law's part, it is true that since the 1970s there has been a shift of emphasis away from the couple relationship towards the regulation of parenting, particularly where families are not co-resident, and that there has been a simultaneous privatisation of the couple relationship, with emphasis on negotiation of the conditions of living together and splitting up. The Human Rights Act 1998 has injected a public element of rights and justice into intimate relations and has led to extensions of marriage to transsexual persons[42] and to recognition of same-sex relationships which are registered.[43] The notion of 'family' may thus appear to have become complex and contested and infinitely extendable, and one way to describe our family living may be as 'chaos'.[44] But when one looks closer at the partnerships and relationships that attract 'family' recognition, there is less scope for diversity than first appears, and law's response can be characterised perhaps less as chaotic[45] than as normalising.[46] Crucially, and particularly in an era of privatisation, this extension of the notion of family serves the economic and social interests of the neo-liberal state.[47]

Statutory provision in family law is now gender neutral, but as we and other contributors highlight, this may obscure its role as a gendering strategy and give rise to 'a search for equivalence' where there is none.[48] Power in both private and public spheres seems to remain resistant to equitable distribution between the sexes, despite the appearance of gender neutrality. It has not been so easy to get away from the symbolic or the material structures of gender. In addition, whereas in the 1970s all women seemed to share a common subordination, it became apparent in the 1990s that differentiation according to economic resources, race, religion and ethnicity make universal claims about the conditions of women difficult to sustain. The modern challenge for feminist family lawyers and for the contributors to this book, therefore, is to reveal the ways in which law is implicated, in the twenty-first century, in all of these complicated, sometimes sophisticated, but always resolute structures of gender.

And so, drawing upon our own recent work and that of other feminist scholars including Martha Fineman and Susan Moller Okin in the US and Brenda

---

40 Neale and Smart (2002), p 196.
41 *Ibid.*
42 Gender Recognition Act 2002.
43 Civil Partnership Act 2004.
44 Beck and Beck-Gernsheim (1995); Dewar (1998); Diduck (2003; 2005).
45 Dewar (1998).
46 Diduck (2003; 2005).
47 Cossman (2002); Boyd and Young (2004); Fineman (2004); Diduck (2005).
48 Collier, Chapter 12; Piper, Chapter 9; Kaganas, Chapter 8.

Cossman, Claire Young and Susan Boyd in Canada, we have grouped contemporary concerns for feminist family law under three headings: autonomy and the shape of identity; equality and equivalence; and familialisation and privatisation. In conceiving of the issues in this way, we and the contributors to this book are indebted to perhaps the greatest legacy that feminist scholarship has left to family law: expanding the range both of what can be known and the questions that can be asked about the world.[49]

What is family law and what does it do?

In positivist terms, family law can be defined as a collection of statutes and cases regulating the family. Such a definition hides more than it reveals, however. Family law can also be said to have a functional role in relation to dispute resolution and the protection of children. It also constitutes some families in particular ways and excludes others.[50] It constitutes individuals in particular ways, as well; it is 'an arena for the ideological struggle over what it means to be a mother, daughter, wife and so forth'.[51] If 'family' has become an ambiguous or at least flexible concept in law, it follows that the concept of family law is also potentially extendable. If family law is about the regulation of what it means to be, and the public or social, as well as the personal, consequences of being, a mother, father, son or daughter, then family law is also employment law,[52] criminal law,[53] youth justice,[54] tax law,[55] immigration law,[56] public and constitutional law,[57] property law,[58] social security law[59] and EU law.[60] In addition, a pluralist approach to law also locates family law in the social as much as in the state,[61] at the level of conscience, feeling and expectations. Family law, as a form of regulation, is about the manipulation of social norms as well as legal ones, and the idea of family law must now grow also to encompass all the ways our family practices are captured by both formal and informal regulation.[62]

In the light of the many roles or functions family law can serve, then, we must try to be as clear as we can about what we want it to do and what we do not want it to have any part in doing. While, for example, many feminists would agree that

---

49 Philipps (2004), p 605.
50 O'Donovan (1993); Diduck and Kaganas (2006).
51 Olsen (1992), p 209.
52 Employment Act 2002; Work and Families Bill 2005.
53 Domestic Violence, Crime and Victims Act 2004, s 5; *A v UK* [1998] 2 FLR 959.
54 Piper, Chapter 9.
55 Mumford, Chapter 10; Philipps (2004); Boyd and Young (2004).
56 Immigration Rules; and see, for a discussion of the concept of family life under Article 8 ECHR, *Singh v Entry Clearance Officer New Delhi* [2004] EWCA Civ 1075.
57 *I v UK* [2002] 2 FLR 518; *Goodwin v UK* [2002] 2 FLR 487.
58 Bottomley and Wong, Chapter 3.
59 See, eg, Jobseeker's Act 1995; New Deal for Lone Parents; New Deal for Partners.
60 *Grant v Southwest Trains* [1998] 1 FLR 839; *Webb v EMO Air Cargo* [1994] ECR 1–03567. See, generally, Salford, 2002.
61 Cotterrell (2002).
62 See O'Donovan (1993); Diduck (2003).

there is some value in law playing some role in encouraging and supporting caring relationships including the care of children, we must remain aware, first, that there is a difference between supporting relationships and supporting only certain acceptable forms of relationships, and second, that family law's concurrent role, 'the public enforcement of private responsibilities of individual family members', acquires a new importance in 'an era of privatization'.[63]

At the same time, while we may wish family law to promote some idea of justice in the 'family' group and ensure that the social, economic and political consequences of belonging to that group are not disproportionately distributed according to gender, generation, sexual orientation, class or culture, we must remain alert to the ways in which feminist ideas of equality or justice may be hijacked in a number of ways. They may, for example, be incorporated into the mainstream where they lose their feminist character.[64] Carol Smart observes how the feminist ethic of care has become transformed 'from a potentially progressive concept into a new form of governance over family life' by its elision with responsible caring in New Labour's family policy agenda.[65] Alternatively, or additionally, feminist ideas may be adopted by those working outside a feminist frame,[66] again, as Smart observes, by fathers who position themselves against mothers and make their claims to fatherhood within a combination of narratives that includes an ethic of care. As Smart states, 'no longer can the ethic of care be seen as a feminist corrective to the influence of the ethic of justice'[67] formerly promoted primarily by fathers and by law and social policy. Feminist ideas may also be hijacked by 'family traditionalists' or by their conversion into claims to formal equality, as Kaganas[68] shows in the context of men's groups' claims to be equal victims of domestic violence.

Family law is, therefore, about the regulation of individuals *and* the regulation of the relationships those individuals form, and one of the tensions inherent in feminist family law is the treatment of the family rather than the individual as the unit of analysis. Looking at both simultaneously, or leaving the choice to persons as to where they situate themselves, seems to be desirable. For feminism this has meant that, while the 'family' is often a closed door behind which power is exercised and abuse takes place, belonging, intimacy and a private life also remain important. And so the critique of family undertaken by feminists in the 1970s was of marriage as an unwritten contract, the terms of which were dictated by male power and upheld by the state through a liberal non-interventionist policy in the private sphere.[69] The feminist response was to open up family and open up silences about intimacy and the individual, about the body, sexuality, emotions, personal identity and private life, and the power of those who draw lines between

---

63 See Diduck (2005); Fineman (2004).
64 Philipps (2004).
65 Chapter 7.
66 Philipps (2004), p 605; Kaganas, Chapter 8; Smart, Chapter 7; Stychin, Chapter 2.
67 Chapter 7.
68 Chapter 8.
69 Weitzman (1981); O'Donovan (1985).

the hidden and the revealed.[70] Much work has been done, therefore, and things are not the same for families as they were even twenty years ago, but there is still much left for family law to do. We hope to continue the project here, by offering tools for analysis of the three themes that preoccupy those in the new millennium who are critical of family law as part of a process of the normalisation or regulation of gendered lives in ways that sustain, rather than expose, the silences.

Issues in family law: (Third wave) feminist concerns[71]

The individual and her autonomy

One of the concerns identified as important in feminist work on families is the way in which particular ideas of individualism, autonomy and agency have been incorporated into family laws. Women's legal autonomy was hard-won by early feminists and is still important, but now it is an autonomy that bears only passing resemblance to the autonomous, 'rational' agents of liberal individualism. Unlike the detached autonomous individual of liberalism, the self in feminist thought is a situated, related and connected self who makes decisions about her life and her self with a rationality that is not exclusively economic. It is a self that not only reacts to situational stimuli, but is created by her situation and her active choices within and constitutive of that situation. This feminist self claims the space to choose who and what to be and to refuse to be confined or contained by structures or meanings about identities.

Anne Barlow and Simon Duncan's[72] work demonstrates how different rationalities may work in making these choices. Often, they say, women with children choose whether or not to engage in paid labour on the basis of more than a simple financial calculation. They exercise a complicated negotiation of moral and economic considerations that are specifically linked to their ideas of being a 'good mother' and belie New Labour's characterisation of them as the economically rational individuals of liberal thought. And Mumford[73] shows that this economically rational individual is also at the heart of tax law, in which the taxable unit is the individual rather than the family and through the way in which the provision of tax credits is given to this unit, government aims to encourage the financial independence of women (as mothers). The problem with the 'rationality mistake' in both these contexts is that it merely encourages women to enter low-paid work and reinforces their dependence upon the male-patterned market, while at the same time discrediting their own moral rationality.

Respecting autonomy may mean understanding the subject from her own perspective. This way forward is advocated by Malik[74] in her approach to a feminist multiculturalism. What Malik shows is how a woman out of tune with her

---

70 Lacey (1998).
71 See also Boyd and Young (2004).
72 Barlow and Duncan (2000).
73 Chapter 10.
74 Chapter 11.

community's traditional norms is caught in a conflict. It is simplistic to argue that she can leave. For minority women, group membership is a critical aspect of their identity. They seek autonomy within the group. The challenge for those who wish to support minority women facing injustice within their family or their community is to strike a balance between showing support and maintaining a critical distance. Malik's chapter is an illuminating example of how a feminist methodology can be crucial to identifying new theoretical and practical concerns. Malik's feminist methodology is to try, so far as this is possible, to see from within the subjectivity of the other.

From this perspective, we can see that differing traditions of family living, including child rearing, may give rise to differing perceptions of justice. We can also see why family law is often central to claims for accommodation made by traditional minorities and consequently why the regulation of women's lives is also central. Women are the reproducers and socialisers of future members of the community, and so it is not only their individual identities which are at stake; the re-creation and maintenance of the collective identity depends upon them. This role may lead to the control of women in relation to sexuality, marriage, divorce and child rearing, and to their bearing a disproportionate burden of any policy of accommodation of cultural or religious practices.

Katherine O'Donovan and Jill Marshall[75] are also concerned about women's autonomy. They make the point that identity is a work in progress and thus stress the importance of the ability to make autonomous choices in shaping that identity. In their argument, the meaning or identity of 'mother' has not been sufficiently challenged, even by feminist scholars. Mother is an identity, they say, that women must be free to remake. And so, while one may argue that much feminist work has already been done to reveal and challenge the 'good mother' of law, the self-sacrificing full-time nurturer of the traditional family,[76] they go further. They argue that women must be free to separate the incidents of motherhood – maternity and mothering – that have for so long been inseverable as one.

Finally, shaping and remaking identity is also a theme in Jones's and Jackson's work. In demonstrating technology's effect upon making families, they demonstrate both the effect it can have upon making family identities and law's resistance to these innovations. They wonder if law's understanding of 'parent' is not fundamentally misguided. Jackson[77] challenges law's continued reliance upon a form of binary reasoning in which one either is or is not a parent and Jones[78] also criticises this dichotomy in her work with lesbian parents, who are often frustrated by the discord between their experience of mothering a child and law's myopia in acknowledging that experience.

---

75 Chapter 6.
76 See, eg, Silva (1996); Diduck (1997); Fineman (1995). Motherhood's association with care and nurture is so ingrained that the lesbian mother is now more acceptable in law than the mother who chooses not to mother. See, for example, discussion in *Re G (Children)* [2006] UKHL 43.
77 Chapter 4.
78 Chapter 5.

Equality and equivalence

In 1974, Finer and McGregor wrote that 'all major developments in family law from [the mid-nineteenth century] onwards' have been directed to 'equality within the law for women [and] equality within the law for people of small means'.[79] In some ways this is true, but while equality always was and still remains an important goal for feminists, it has become a disputed concept. Formal equality or sameness of treatment may have been the goal of first-wave feminists, but since then feminist theorising about equality has shifted enormously. Many feminists have, for example, criticised sameness of treatment as reinforcing a norm which might be better disputed. Formal equality resolves only the 'problem' of treating people or situations differently; it does not redress dominance, nor does it always recognise that different treatment may sometimes be required to compensate for disadvantage created by institutions or structural conditions.

Finer and McGregor may be correct, however, at least to the extent that the language of equality or equal treatment has become important in family law.[80] As Stychin observes, for example, formal equality was a driving principle behind the passage of the Civil Partnership Act 2004. As he also observes, however, the Act fits precisely within New Labour's 'third way' political discourse and can be seen as much as a method of disciplining family living as a celebration of 'alternative' family living. Arguing that same-sex partnerships are 'the same' as heterosexual married ones can thus serve to marginalise and 'other' those who wish to live outside the family norm while remaining within the politically acceptable discourse of equality.

Christine Piper also observes the ways in which gender neutrality, or formal equality, operate to the disadvantage of young girls and women. Young female offenders are different from young male offenders in their backgrounds and in the offences they commit, yet the expectations of and responses by the authorities are all 'gender neutral'. Rather than resulting in equality and justice for all young offenders, however, Piper shows how sameness of treatment simply renders girls invisible to the youth justice system. They are subsumed under the category 'youth'. Piper asks the 'woman question' in the context of youth justice policy, and sees it failing young girls and women.

Equality has also resurfaced as an important standard by which to judge relations between individual members of the family itself. While treating fathers and mothers equally in custody disputes was a goal for early feminists who campaigned against the patriarchal system of 'father right',[81] formal equality between parents seemed to fall out of favour in the mid-twentieth century. As the reality of gendered roles in child care during cohabitation were given legal recognition in residence and contact arrangements on separation, feminist concern shifted to ensuring that women and children were not financially or socially disadvantaged by those arrangements, and it has been fathers who have regenerated claims for

---

79 Finer and McGregor (1974), p 101.
80 Diduck and Kaganas (2006).
81 *Ibid*; Maidment (1984).

parents to be treated equally. To feminists it is clear, though, that formal equality for mothers in the nineteenth century was a different claim and had different effects from fathers claims for formal equality in the twenty-first century. Further, achieving a form of equality in the distribution of the financial consequences of family living is also a goal that law has adopted. But, again, this form of equality too often has resulted in disadvantage for women. Let us consider the movement toward equality, or equivalence, in both financial matters and child-care matters.

One area regularly written about in feminist legal theory is the plight of the single mother. Where she has gone through divorce 'precipitous downward mobility both economically and socially'[82] was identified as the outcome. This was partially due to applying principles of formal equality to women who were economically dependent upon their husbands during marriage.[83] The English courts now appear to have parted company with those in the United States by attempting an equal valuing of roles in marriage, whether as primary carer or wage earner. Indeed, the decisions in *White v White*[84] and *Miller v Miller; McFarlane v McFarlane*[85] mark an effort by the judiciary to bring some substantive, rather than merely formal, equality into post-divorce financial provision. Together, these cases introduce into the objective of 'fairness' the recognition of family work as work of equal significance with market work, non-discrimination between husband and wife as a 'principle of universal application' and the need for compensation for economic disparity arising from the way the parties organised their family lives, including, but not exclusively, their responsibility for the (pre- and post-divorce) care of children. But even these apparently progressive decisions may be only symbolic for the majority of single mothers, as they apply only to families with sufficient assets to share. For most single mothers, the failures of the Child Support Agency to ensure financial help in raising children remain a national scandal.[86]

Further, as Susan Boyd has recognised, compensation of a woman's unpaid labour in the home is only achieved if she has a former husband or civil partner against whom to make her claim. The benefit that all of society receives by the unpaid labour of a woman without a (former) partner, or by one who does not wish to make a claim against him or her, is thus neither recognised nor compensated, and 'ideologically, heterosexual relationships – and women's roles as wives and mothers within them – are thus reproduced'.[87]

It is arguable that the rhetoric of formal equality has been taken also into discussions of parenting.[88] We see it operating in recent amendments to the Children Act 1989, which give fathers parental responsibility over their non-marital children, and in the new 'truth' that the welfare of children demands that

---

82 Weitzman (1981), p 323.
83 See, for example, the Supreme Court of Canada's remarks in *Moge v Moge* [1992] 3 SCR 813.
84 *White v White* [2001] 1 AC 596.
85 [2006] UKHL 24.
86 *R v Secretary of State for Work and Pensions ex parte Kehoe* [2005] UKHL 48.
87 Boyd (1994), p 69.
88 Diduck and Kaganas (2006), ch 7.

(arguably only) at the end of their parents' relationships, fathers should be assumed to be equal carers.

Twenty-four per cent of children live in a lone-parent household; nine out of ten of these live with their mothers. Of the 76 per cent of children in households headed by a couple, not all are living with both birth parents. Of children living in a stepfamily household, 83 per cent live with a stepfather.[89] Thus children are most likely to encounter family law through contact and divorce cases, and these cases are most likely to concern claims by fathers. Kaganas examines discourses utilised by some fathers' groups who consider the courts to discriminate in favour of mothers. They deploy the discourse of formal equality or equivalence in debates about domestic violence, but Kaganas argues that use of this discourse may merely be a strategy employed to control their ex-partners and children while relieving them of the need to resort to unacceptable patriarchal claims to do so. Just as in the financial provision cases that do not involve 'big money', we can see in Kaganas's work how women may be hurt by the hard choices they make between family work and market work, and that men's specialisation in market work may hurt men also when it comes to remaining part of their children's active families.

Smart argues also that a new narrative of fatherhood, based on claims to care as well as to justice and rights, repositions the father within the post-separation family. Her suggestion is that although some fathers may engage in gendered blaming and a denigration of motherhood, others express an emergent change in how fathers wish to relate to their children. This links to Collier's analysis of the deconstruction of masculinities and femininities in academic debates. He argues that models of both genders are outdated and that gender identities are in the process of being freed up. What is needed is a return in feminist theory to material conditions, where issues of power, interest and political economy are central. The contribution of post-modernist feminist debates has been to create awareness of the diversity of family forms and practices, and of identities as performed. Smart's and Collier's work here highlights the importance of bringing together insights on creating identities and exclusions with an analysis of material inequalities in the relative positions of women and men, as a way forward from debates about formal equality.

Familial ideology, familialisation and privatisation

While the theme of equality runs through family law, it is almost paradoxical that, at the same time, the families to which this principle is applied retain their normative, status-based traditionalism. As Stychin and Bottomley and Wong point out, they are still dyadic and (usually) sexual relationships. They are economically self-sufficient and are said to be entered into by choice. And so, while there has been a movement in family law to extend the notion of 'family' beyond its traditional limits, same-sex relationship recognition was achieved in part because these relationships were argued to be 'the same' as marriage relationships, and unmarried

---

89 Office for National Statistics, *Social Trends 2005*, Tables 2.4, 2.10, 2.13.

or unregistered cohabitation soon may be attributed with some legal rights and obligations partly for the same reason.[90] The extension of the notion of the marriage-like 'family', to *stabilise and discipline* relationships, has been a recurrent theme in much feminist work on family law[91] and is considered here by Bottomley and Wong and by Stychin in the context of adult relationships.[92]

Jones also demonstrates that, while family status may be extended to same-sex parents, law has not conceded a name for those parents; parenthood remains framed through a hetero-normative lens. And with the advent of new medical technologies, the question 'who are the parents?' has become ever more complex. Jackson argues that cell nuclear replacement, which takes genetic parenthood beyond the union of female and male gametes, requires us to rethink the exclusivity of 'one mother/one father' taking the familialisation project into entirely new territory.

Notwithstanding these difficulties with parenthood, the familialisation of society – that is, the ever-increasing range of relationships that are captured within the regulatory net – continues apace, and because the net retains its traditional contours, familialisation has profound and gendered consequences. It can be seen as a part of New Labour's neo-liberal modernisation project, which includes a re-ordering of the ways in which responsibility not only is exercised, but is felt or conceived. In this project, one's responsibility to society, usually called the taxpayer, and even one's responsibility to self is increasingly framed within the discourse of family. Familialisation thus affects one's economic and social responsibilities as much as it does one's personal ones.

In Canada, Judy Fudge and Brenda Cossman say that there is a whole new set of assumptions about the role of government and the rights of citizens:

> In the new political and social order, governments are no longer responsible for the social welfare of their citizens but only for helping those citizens to help themselves. The social citizen is giving way to the market citizen who (quoting Brodie, 1996) 'recognizes the limits and liabilities of state provision and embraces her obligation to become more self-reliant'. This new market citizen recognizes and takes responsibility for her own risk and that of her family.[93]

Within this frame, old certainties become re-ordered. Formerly social or political problems become recast as private, family problems, solvable by individual family members. Child poverty, for example, could be solved if non-resident parents simply acted responsibly and paid their child support.[94] Unemployment can be solved by reframing the 'good' of employment less as a social one than as a matter of the welfare of one's child,[95] which adds a new perspective to Mumford's work on child tax credits as a means of encouraging mothers into low-paid work. The

---

90 Barlow *et al* (2005); Law Commission (2006).

91 See, eg, Smart (1984); Cossman and Ryder (2001); Day Sclater and Piper (2000); Diduck (2005).

92 See also Diduck (2005), who argues that this extension also disciplines society.

93 Fudge and Cossman (2002), p 16.

94 HM Treasury (2004) *Child Poverty Review*.

95 *Ibid*.

problems of youth crime and disaffected youth generally can be solved if parents accept appropriate parenting training, are employed outside the home and take responsibility for their children's criminal, anti-social and truanting behaviour.[96] Myriad social problems, it seems, can be solved by people simply taking their *family* responsibilities seriously. But, as we have seen, a disproportionate burden for meeting these privatised social responsibilities lies upon women as carers and workers. Piper notes both the privatisation and the gender of these responsibilities in the context of juvenile justice. In remarking upon the elision of civil/family justice with criminal/youth justice, she recognises a policy trend to support or discipline the family 'as a means of strengthening the moral basis for an ordered society',[97] and that 'more children are being drawn into an increasingly important system in which the risk of offending normally takes priority over the risk of harm, or the latter risk is subsumed into the former'.[98] She also notes that 80 per cent of offenders are males and 80 per cent of parents sanctioned with parenting orders are mothers. Fathers do not seem to play a significant role.

Familialisation thus can be argued to be an important means of diverting responsibility for the welfare of society and its members from the state to individual families. It is also a means by which the state can deflect responsibility for the economic well-being of individual citizens.

> It is the family, not the state or the market, that assumes responsibility for both the inevitable dependent – the child or other biologically or developmentally dependent person – and the derivative dependent – the caretaker. The institution of the family operates structurally and ideologically to free markets from considering or accommodating dependency. The state is cast as a default institution, providing minimal, grudging and stigmatized assistance should families fail.[99]

And so, as the economic and social consequences of care and dependency are increasingly privatised, we see a shift in the balance of responsibility for the costs of social reproduction from the state to the 'family' and its individual members.[100] The implications of this shift for dependants, usually women and the children they care for, are serious because it is happening at the same time as the welfare state is being dismantled and the other concurrent structural changes which would assist them in assuming responsibility, such as job security and child care, lag far behind.[101] Familial ideology is powerful, and its implications are great for women in the current climate of privatisation.

Conclusions

Feminism's impact on family law has been mixed; almost paradoxical. Recent legal reform and the contributions to this collection illustrate this ambiguity. They

---

96 Piper, Chapter 9.
97 Chapter 9.
98 Chapter 9.
99 Fineman (2004), p 228.
100 Fudge and Cossman (2002), p 28.
101 Cossman (2002), p 169.

show, for example, that families or legal partnerships may now be formed by people of the same sex and legal parenthood may now be held by people of the same sex; that the employment world and the tax–benefit system make provision for parenthood; that the language of care has become acceptable in legal discourse; and that law can pay real attention to different aspects, including cultural aspects, of identity. In other words, they show that identities – or legal subjectivities – are changeable; that family practices do occur outside the home; that a moral and ethical voice can be heard by law; and that our subjectivities are made as much by our context and connections as they are by our natures. These are all feminist ideas.

And even where feminist ideas have not resulted directly in legal change, they may have laid the groundwork for progressive dialogue to occur among policy and law makers and they have certainly created space for conversations among academics, activists and practitioners. Feminism may also have had some influence at the micro level in how family life is lived at home or within individual places of work, affecting gender performances on a daily basis. And even where feminist perspectives have not influenced a majority of the court so as to be counted as a 'win', they may open that area of law to future analysis, all the more strongly if they are referred to in the reasons of the minority.[102]

Yet, on the other hand, law's resistance to feminist concerns remains strong. The underlying principles of English law mean that as much as one's legal subjectivity has changed over the years, particularly women's and children's legal subjectivity, family law either denies that changeability and pronounces the changed situation to be simply the situation that always was (as in *R v R*), or acknowledges it in ways which serve particular, sometimes anti-feminist, interests. It is consistent with current social and economic policy for all adults, even mothers, to take up paid employment, and so, with all adults now encouraged to be parent-workers, maternity, paternity and parenting leave laws make economic sense, as does the adoption of equality principles in parenting disputes. And while feminist goals of disrupting and problematising legal norms have extended ideas of family, they have not yet disrupted the (sexual) couple or the one-mother-one-father model of family, often with disheartening effects on individuals.

The same ambivalence can be seen in family law's use of the liberal principle of equality. While non-discrimination and equality have a place in feminist discourse, and legal innovations such as the equal valuing of an increasing range of caring relationships or of financial contributions and unpaid labour to those relationships can be seen as progressive, they also reinforce a particular gendered norm of family living. That norm serves to disadvantage dependants of limited financial means within the unit, as well as all those living outside it. We see here how feminist concerns of equality, non-discrimination, care and subjectivity can be adopted to further agendas which may not be feminist at all. Feminism has not yet succeeded in adequately challenging the ideology of the family, which has such profound material consequences for women's and children's economic well-being.

---

102 Philipps (2004), p 606.

The feminisation of poverty continues and may in fact be reinforced by the rhetoric of equality and choice.

What a feminist perspective may reveal at the beginning of the twenty-first century, however, is that law contains the conceptual tools to promote feminist principles, even while resistance to using them remains strong. Structures of power/gender are difficult to shift. And so feminist activism to reform or transform the law must continue, but, importantly, feminist theory must also continue its journey into understanding how gender is 'done', how it is constructed, deconstructed, made, remade and performed on a day-to-day basis.

Our twenty-first-century feminist perspective may also reveal that the nature or method of law's regulation of family life is changing. We said above that family law has always been about the regulation of family responsibilities and family identities inside and outside the home. But while even fifty years ago that regulation took the form of direct prohibition or prescription of conduct, or of appeal to an absolute and assumedly consensus-based morality, much of the new regulation – the new family law – regulates by means of the normalisation of individual and social attitudes as much as individual and social conduct. We are encouraged, informed and educated to become good familial/social citizens.[103] On the one hand, the boundary between the public–private divide seems to have been breached, yet on the other, it seems only to have shifted as we make our familial selves and our families in this new context, in which our calls for respect for autonomy only appear to have been heard. Rooted in the rhetoric of choice, and located in the ethic of self-responsibility and equality with others, normalisation aims to make a good society by making good families. The feminist project must continue to be to recognise and challenge different forms of legal regulation so as to ensure that the good society and good families are good for all, including women and children regardless of their sexuality, economic means or ethnicity.

References

Barlow, A and Duncan, S (2000) 'New Labour's communitarianism, supporting families and the "rationality mistake": Part I', 22(2) *J of Social Welfare and Family Law* 23

Barlow, A, Duncan, S, James, G and Park, A (2005) *Cohabitation, Marriage and the Law*, Oxford: Hart

Beck, U and Beck-Gernsheim, E (1995) *The Normal Chaos of Love*, Cambridge: Polity

Boyd, S (1994) '(Re)Placing the State: Family, law and oppression', 9 *Canadian J of Law and Society* 39

Boyd, S and Young, C (2004) 'Feminism, law, and public policy: Family feuds and taxing times', 42 *Osgoode Hall LJ* 545

103 See Reece (2003); Diduck (2003).

Chodorow, N (1978) *The Reproduction of Mothering: Psychoanalysis and the Sociology of Gender*, Berkeley, CA: University of California

Collier, R (2001) 'A hard time to be a father? Reassessing the relationship between law, policy and family (practices)', 28 *J of Law and Society* 520

Cossman, B (2002) 'Family feuds: Neo-conservative and neo-liberal visions of the Reprivatization Project', in Fudge, J and Cossman, B (eds) *Privatization, Law and the Challenge to Feminism*, Toronto: University of Toronto Press

Cossman, B and Ryder, B (2001) 'What is marriage-like like? The irrelevance of conjugality', 18 *Canadian J of Family Law* 269

Cotterrell, R (2002) 'Subverting orthodoxy, making law central: A view of socio-legal studies' 29 *J of Law and Society* 632

Day Sclater, S and Piper, C (2000) 'Remoralising the family? – Family policy, family law and youth justice' 12 *Child and Family Law Quarterly* 135

Dewar, J (1998) 'The normal chaos of family law', 61(4) *Modern Law Review* 467

Diduck, A (1997) 'In search of the feminist good mother', 7 *Social and Legal Studies* 129

Diduck, A (2003) *Law's Families*, Cambridge: Cambridge University Press

Diduck, A (2005) 'Shifting familiarity', 58 *Current Legal Problems* 235

Diduck, A and Kaganas, F (2006) *Family Law, Gender and the State*, 2nd edn, Oxford: Hart

Douglas, S and Michaels, M (2004) *The Mommy Myth: The Idealization of Motherhood and How it Has Undermined Women*, New York: Free Press

Fineman, M (1995) *The Neutered Mother, The Sexual Family and Other Twentieth Century Tragedies*, London: Routledge

Fineman, M (2004) *The Autonomy Myth*, New York: The New Press

Finer, M and McGregor, O (1974) 'History of the obligation to maintain', Appendix 5, in Finer, M, *Report of the Committee on One Parent Families*, London: HMSO Cmnd 5629

Fudge, J and Cossman, B (2002) 'Introduction: Privatization, law and the challenge to feminism', in Fudge, J and Cossman, B (eds) *Privatization, Law and the Challenge to Feminism*, Toronto: University of Toronto Press

HM Treasury (2004) *Child Poverty Review*

Lacey, N (1998) *Unspeakable Subjects*, Oxford: Hart Publishing

Law Commission (2006) *Consultation Paper No 179: Cohabitation: The Financial Consequences of Relationship Breakdown*, London

Maidment, S (1984) *Child Custody and Divorce: The Law in Social Context*, London: Croom Helm

Morgan, DHJ (1996) *Family Connections*, Cambridge: Polity Press

Neale, B and Smart, C (2002) 'Caring, earning and changing: Parenthood and employment after divorce', in Carling, A, Duncan, S and Edwards, R (eds) *Analysing Families: Morality and Rationality in Policy and Practice*, London: Routledge

O'Donovan, K (1985) *Sexual Divisions in Law*, London: Weidenfeld

O'Donovan, K (1993) *Family Law Matters*, London: Pluto

Okin, S (1989) *Justice, Gender and the Family*, New York: Basic Books

Olsen, F (1992) 'Children's rights: Some feminist approaches to the United Nations Convention on the Rights of the Child', in Alston, P, Parker, S and Seymour, J (eds) *Children, Rights and the Law*, Oxford: Clarendon Press

Philipps, L (2004) 'Measuring the effects of feminist legal research: Looking critically at "failure" and "success" ', 42 *Osgoode Hall LJ* 603

Reece, H (2003) *Divorcing Responsibly*, Oxford: Hart Publishing

Salford, H (2002) 'Concepts of family under EU Law – Lessons from the ECHR', 16 *International J of Law, Policy and the Family* 410

Silva, EB (1996) *Good Enough Mothering? Feminist Perspectives on Lone Motherhood*, London and New York: Routledge

Smart, C (1984) *The Ties that Bind*, London: Routledge and Keegan Paul

Smart, C (1989) *Feminism and the Power of Law*, London: Routledge

Weitzman, L (1981) *The Marriage Contract*, New York: Free Press

Chapter 2

Family Friendly? Rights, Responsibilities and Relationship Recognition
Carl Stychin

Introduction

> It would be odd indeed if those who espouse and defend traditional values of com-
> mitment and faithfulness opposed giving gay couples the choice to live their lives
> according to those values.[1]

Families are changing. I suspect that teachers of family law have been uttering
those words to their students for more years than most lecturers care to remember.
Yet within the United Kingdom today, we are witnessing an unprecedented
change in the way in which some families are characterised within political and
legal discourse. Over the last twenty years, lesbian and gay families have been transformed. Not in the sense that the actual forms that their families take necessarily
have altered; rather, what has changed so significantly is the way in which those
families are characterised and comprehended within politics, the media, and the
law. In the 1980s, lesbians and gays were (in)famously described as forming
'pretended family relationships', which should not be 'promoted' by local government.[2] This political delegitimation of relationships was profoundly demeaning
to many, underscoring the social and psychological significance of the term
'family' within Western society. Ironically, however, that Conservative political
tactic galvanised the lesbian and gay movement in the UK, which responded by
articulating the richness of lesbian and gay families in the public sphere.

By 2004, much had changed. The Civil Partnership Act was enacted by Parliament, with overwhelming support, including from most of the Conservative front
benches. Even opponents of the Act seemed to accept that lesbian and gay people
form loving relationships that deserve respect and protection from a range of
injustices. For the government, the Act represents the culmination of the quest
for equality, creating a legal status for same-sex couples from which most of the
benefits (and responsibilities) of marriage will flow. Lesbian and gay partnership is
no longer, then, a pretend family form. Rather, it is a form of family warranting
equal respect and dignity because of its value to individuals and to society. For
those who have lived through the previous two decades, it is quite a remarkable
journey from pretend family to civil partnership. The purpose of this chapter is to
consider critically where that journey has now brought lesbians and gay men in
Britain, and whether we reached quite the destination at which we hoped our
journey would end.

To place the legislation in a wider political context, it is fair to say that the
Labour government can point to a range of legislative and other initiatives, since
its first election to government in 1997, which suggest that the Civil Partnership

---

1 *Hansard*, Commons, 12 October 2004, p 190: Mr Alan Duncan (Conservative).
2 Local Government Act 1988 s 28.

Act is in keeping with a 'gay-friendly' agenda. Certainly, the website of the Women and Equality Unit provides ample 'spin' for this claim.[3] As a result of the Adoption and Children Act 2002, same-sex couples can apply to adopt a child jointly. Other examples include the availability of paternity leave and flexible working hours to a same-sex partner; a right to register a death of a same-sex partner; since December 2003, anti-discrimination legislation tackles discrimination in employment and training on grounds of sexual orientation and religion (legislation which is a legal requirement for Member States of the European Union); new sexual offences legislation removes discrimination between men and women, and between those of different sexual orientations; s 28 of the Local Government Act 1988 has been repealed after much difficulty in the House of Lords (although replaced with guidance to schools, which states that 'there should be no direct promotion of sexual orientation'[4]); the age of consent has been reduced to 16 for gay men; the Criminal Injuries Compensation Scheme now includes same-sex partners; and the immigration rules have been amended to improve the situation for same-sex partners. Although many of these changes, it can be argued, fall short of perfection, they do represent a significant and real change from the many years of Conservative Party rule.

The Civil Partnership Act is seen by many as the culmination of this programme of reform. Put simply, the legislation

> creates a new legal status that would allow adult same-sex couples to gain formal recognition of their relationship. Same-sex couples who enter a civil partnership would access a wide range of rights and responsibilities, reflecting the important commitment they are making to one another.[5]

This bundle of rights and responsibilities includes: the duty to provide reasonable maintenance for a civil partner; the duty to provide reasonable maintenance for children of the family; assessment in the same way as spouses for child support purposes; equitable treatment for the purposes of life assurance; employment and pension benefits;[6] recognition under intestacy rules;[7] access to fatal accidents compensation; protection from domestic violence; and recognition for

---

3   www.womenandequalityunit.gov.uk/lgbt/key_facts.htm: Angela Mason, who led the campaign at Stonewall for the Civil Partnership Act, later became the head of the Women and Equality Unit.

4   These guidelines were issued on 7 July 2000.

5   www.womenandequalityunit.gov.uk/lgbt/partnership.htm.

6   The pension questions raised by the Act are complex and not entirely resolved. In particular, the issue of pension provision for dependent surviving civil partners remains a contentious issue. The argument that the survivor partner's pension should be based upon *all* of the deceased's pension contributions, and not just those made since the coming into force of the Civil Partnership Act, has not been accepted by the government. Further announcements are promised from the government on the pension implications of partnership.

7   The ability to transfer property upon death free from inheritance tax has proven to be one of the most controversial areas of debate, leading to wider questions regarding why same-sex couples should be financially 'privileged' in this way over other dependent relationships. It has also led to debate regarding the relative merits of inheritance tax more generally; an interesting question which is beyond the scope of this chapter.

immigration and nationality purposes. Couples are allowed to enter a civil partnership through a statutory civil registration procedure. A dissolution process – a formal procedure in the courts – will be created which mirrors divorce (rather than a simple ending of a contract unilaterally or bilaterally). In sum, according to the Women and Equality Unit: 'Access to a civil partnership would bring benefits to the individuals who enter them, and benefits for society as a whole. Civil partnership underlines the inherent value of committed same-sex relationships, supports stable families and shows that we value the diversity of the society we live in.'[8]

The Bill was introduced in the House of Lords, receiving its third reading on 1 July 2004. In that process, however, it was amended to extend its coverage to family members and 'carers' more generally who might wish to register and opt into the bundle of rights and responsibilities. The Bill then moved to the House of Commons, and that amendment (as well as other similar attempts to amend the legislation in order to expand its scope: for example, to siblings) was defeated. The Bill received its third reading in the House of Commons on 9 November 2004, receiving broad parliamentary support. The Commons amendments were approved by the House of Lords on 17 November 2004, and the Bill received Royal Assent the following day, making it law: the Civil Partnership Act 2004. It is now in force.

'Parallel but different'?

Arguably, the ingeniousness of the Civil Partnership Act is the fact that it can produce a legal status of 'civil partner' that does not depend upon marriage, but which displays virtually all of the characteristics of a civil marriage. This is undoubtedly a strategy on the part of the government to avoid what it perceives as the likelihood of backlash to same-sex marriage in the UK. At the same time, it can fulfil its promise of equality by granting a legal status to committed same-sex couples. The government is strongly on record throughout its term of office as supportive of the institution of marriage for opposite-sex couples – as helping to foster stable relationships and as the best means to raise children – and civil partnership provides an alternative, politically saleable route for same-sex couples. The social benefits that marriage offers can be furthered through civil partnership, while avoiding the criticism that same-sex unions undermine the institution of marriage. As Labour Baroness Scotland made clear during the debate:

> This Bill does not undermine or weaken the importance of marriage and we do not propose to open civil partnership to opposite-sex couples. Civil partnership is aimed at same-sex couples who cannot marry. . . . We continue to support marriage and recognise that it is the surest foundation for opposite-sex couples raising children.[9]

The stable couple form, it is argued, is good for the individual, for the couple, and for society (and the economy) as a whole. Long-term, traditional, stable,

---

8   www.womenandequalityunit.gov.uk/lgbt/partnership.htm.
9   *Hansard*, Lords, 22 April 2004, p 388, Baroness Scotland (Labour).

legally recognised relationships thus become the socially preferred option. Marriage is the ideal, but civil partnership – for those unable to marry – becomes an alternative which can further the same social policy goals. As the Government Minister Jacqui Smith explained in the House of Commons:

> [W]e seek to create a parallel but different legal relationship that mirrors as fully as possible the rights and responsibilities enjoyed by those who can marry, and that uses civil marriage as a template for the processes, rights and responsibilities that go with civil partnership. We are doing this for reasons of equality and social justice.[10]

Opponents of civil partnership, not surprisingly, argue that the Act creates 'a parody of marriage for homosexual couples'.[11] It is same-sex marriage in all but name. Moreover, the challenge offered by critics of the Act is itself ingenious. That is, if this is not marriage, then surely it is a status that should be available to others similarly situated to lesbian and gay couples, namely, all those who care for each other in an interdependent, committed relationship. Otherwise, those individuals (and groups of people, such as home sharers) are discriminated against by this legislation. When that argument is rejected by government, opponents can forcefully claim that this is a status that is marriage in all but name (and vows).

In order to bolster the argument in favour of the extension of civil partnerships to carers, friends, spinsters and spinster sisters, opponents of the Act, as it was introduced by the government, argued that the basis of the legislation should be explicitly contractual. Partnership, they claimed, should focus on recognising and supporting agreements between people to live intertwined, interdependent lives, and the state should provide its support to all such agreements. On this point, an amendment was made in the House of Lords to replace the term 'relationship' with 'contract', as part of the wider strategy of amendment to include carers, siblings and other dependent relationships. In this way, opponents hoped that the limitation within the Act to same-sex assumed sexual relationships would be rendered more difficult to sustain. If civil partnership is not marriage, then what can it be except a domestic contract? If so, then surely *anyone* can contract, including spinster sisters (or, for that matter, more than two people).

This argument has much logic. This *does* look like civil marriage in all but name designed to extend the perceived social benefits of marriage to an (assumed) clearly delineated group who most closely resemble married couples. There is no religious element (by law), and there is no possibility for an 'official' ceremony. But, even here, the material produced by the government encourages same-sex couples to plan little (or, one might imagine, lavish) ceremonies to mark the registration. One side benefit, mentioned in the Regulatory Impact Assessment that accompanies the legislation, is that with registration there 'can be expected . . . a small increase in demand for the hospitality industry as the result of couples entering civil partnership choosing to hold a form of celebration in a similar vein to a wedding reception'.[12]

---

10 *Hansard*, Commons, 9 November 2004, p 776, Ms Jacqui Smith (Labour).
11 *Hansard*, Lords, 22 April 2004, p 405, Baroness O'Cathain (Conservative).
12 Department of Trade and Industry (DTI) (2004), p 22.

The conservative critique of the Civil Partnership Act is not wholly dissimilar to criticism of the legislation that can be offered from a more progressive or even radical perspective. The argument from this side of the spectrum is that if the state is going to proceed to recognise relationship forms outside of the institution of marriage, then it is an ideal opportunity to think about *alternatives* to the marriage model that might better reflect the diversity of relationship forms that exist. Such a rethink might also be an opportunity to come to terms with the feminist and other critiques of the institution of marriage which have been made forcefully for many years.[13] In other words, rather than extending marriage (in all but name), perhaps we should have thought about creating legal alternatives to marriage (open to all). However, this is explicitly rejected by government in quite a conservative fashion, through the (highly debatable) claim that such an approach might weaken the institution of marriage, which, it is assumed, would be a socially deleterious outcome.

An attempt at creating an alternative framework can be found in the Private Member's Bill introduced in the House of Lords by Lord Lester (and subsequently withdrawn) in 2003. Lord Lester's Bill was an attempt to produce an alternative, universally available model open to same-sex and opposite-sex couples. The Bill was particularly notable for the extent to which it moved away from the marriage model, allowing greater financial autonomy for couples during a relationship and on breakdown, including through contractual arrangements agreed in advance. It also created a simple no-fault procedure on breakdown, based on a two-month unilateral notice period. The Bill could be interpreted as a move away from status towards autonomy, contract, and reasonable expectations in relationships, to be negotiated and agreed by the parties, as well as easy exit (which is specifically rejected by the government in the context of marriage and partnership). There were other interesting innovations offered by Lord Lester, including a commitment period of cohabitation required before registration. The availability of this form of legal partnership to all cohabiting couples no matter what genders is particularly significant in that it would have created an alternative to marriage available to all, but which (unlike the Civil Partnership Act) was linked to cohabitation as a requirement.

For those who advocate this approach, the Civil Partnership Act can be seen as disappointing. It is the creation of a new status (in an old wedding dress) available to same-sex couples, but not opposite-sex couples, for whom it is marriage or nothing. For those heterosexual couples for whom marriage as an institution is unappealing (for personal, ideological or other reasons), this particular bundle of rights and responsibilities is not available. However, as it is virtually a marriage in all but name, it provides no real alternative anyway. Thus, an opportunity has been lost for radical reform in the family law area.

Politically, then, some liberals may view the Civil Partnership Act as a denial of equality of access to the status of marriage, rejecting the 'parallel but different' approach. Some conservatives (and radicals) see the Act as unfairly limited in its

---

13 See, eg, O'Donovan (1993); Auchmuty (2004).

scope to those who define as a 'homosexual couple', rather than being available to others who share interconnected lives, for whom there is no status currently on offer. The Act thereby may prove to be either a clever means of satisfying the gay 'constituency' while avoiding the alienation of 'middle England', or a strategy which does not completely please anyone at all.

The Third Way?

No matter what one's view of the political implications of the Act (if, indeed, it even registers on the political radar in a significant way), the contours of the Civil Partnership Act should not come as a surprise to any observer of New Labour ideology. I have elsewhere tried to understand New Labour's ideological construction of lesbian and gay sexualities, and I have identified six key elements of New Labour's 'Third Way' discourse:

- the centrality of the idea (and ideal) of social inclusion (as opposed to economic equality and redistribution);
- the linking of rights and responsibilities: the enjoyment of rights as being conditioned upon the acceptance of (moral) responsibilities as citizens;
- the importance of community as performing the key function of inculcating the values of citizenship, social inclusion, and the social control of deviant behaviour;
- the importance of the family in producing responsible, active new citizens, and as providing a counterbalance to rugged individualism and atomisation;
- the desirability of consensus within One Nation in which acceptance of multiculturalism and tolerance of 'difference' (within limits) prevails;
- a faith in managerialism and law, in which social problems can be solved through the state and through law.[14]

The Civil Partnership Act, I want now to argue, can be located squarely within this set of Third Way characteristics.

Social inclusion

An examination of the explanatory material produced by the Women and Equality Unit reveals, first, a strong justification for registered partnerships to be found in the importance of *social inclusion*. The Final Regulatory Impact Assessment emphasises that this is one of the benefits of partnership registration, and a causal connection between law and social change is also clearly drawn. The reform of the law is linked to social attitudes around inclusion and exclusion:

> The Government believes that the creation of a new legal status for same-sex couples would play an important role in increasing social acceptance of same-sex relationships, reducing homophobia and discrimination and building a safer and

---

14 Stychin (2003), ch 2. See also, eg, Bell and Binnie (2000); Carabine and Monro (2004); McGhee (2003); Powell (2000); Rose (2000); Sevenhuijsen (2000); Williams and Roseneil (2004).

more inclusive society . . . Legislation will act as an important step in publicly valuing same-sex relationships . . . it will be much harder for people to ignore this commitment both in law and in everyday life. The Government believes that by making a public declaration of their commitment, lesbian, gay and bisexual people will feel more confident that their relationships will be respected and appreciated by society. It is not acceptable that same-sex couples still have to struggle to have their families recognised and the creation of a civil partnership scheme will be a way through which society acknowledges and values their relationships.[15]

Moreover, social inclusion is inseparable within Third Way ideology from the economic, and specifically the idea of economic inclusion through paid employment or entrepreneurship. To be in paid work is to be part of the social, and to not be in paid employment is to have exited the social. The social and the economic become largely coterminous, and there is little value added to society if the individual is not in work (with the possible exception of full-time carers and, to a much lesser extent, stay-at-home parents).

This logic is demonstrated by the economic benefits that will allegedly flow from the Act, as explained in the Regulatory Impact Assessment:

It is hoped that businesses would see improvements in recruitment and retention from offering equal employee benefits to same-sex partners in civil partnership. Recent research by Stonewall into the attitudes of lesbian, gay and bisexual graduates found that equality of terms, conditions and benefits was one of the key factors for organisations to focus on if they were to attract high calibre lesbian, gay and bisexual employees. The Government estimates there to be between 1.5 and 2 million lesbian, gay and bisexual people in the labour force. Through the contribution to wider equality that civil partnership makes, businesses may therefore benefit by being able to draw from a wider pool of talent, and therefore attract and retain a higher calibre of staff from a range of backgrounds.[16]

Not only will social inclusion be enhanced, but we will approach something closer to an economic state of perfect efficiency, as human capital moves to where it is most highly valued. The social and the economic thus squarely meet.

Opponents of the Act in Parliament do force the government to confront the position of carers, and the citizenship value of care giving (rather than paid employment), in making the claim that the remit of the Civil Partnership Act should be extended to others. In this way, the debates usefully bring care giving and the paucity of public benefits for carers into the public, parliamentary realm. However, the government clearly rejected the vehicle of the Civil Partnership Act as a way to improve the lot of the carers more generally, falling back on the analogy between same-sex and married couples.

Rights and responsibilities

The theme of rights and responsibilities runs throughout the Act, the commentary that surrounds it and the parliamentary debates. The Act itself is characterised

---

15 DTI (2004), pp 16–17.
16 *Ibid*, p 22.

as 'a package of rights and responsibilities'[17] and as aiming to 'balance the responsibilities of caring for and maintaining a partner with a package of rights for example, in the area of inheritance'.[18] This ideal of balance – between, for example, care and money – is prevalent in the explanatory material. The explicit logic is that one does not receive rights without the taking on of responsibilities. Moreover, the implicit assumption is that one will be less likely to take on responsibilities towards others (such as care) unless rights are accrued. We find here a very utilitarian notion of rights and responsibilities in which the two are almost quantifiable and measurable to achieve a perfect balance. As the government makes clear: 'The registration of a civil partnership involves both legal obligations as well as legal protections. It would not be appropriate for couples to gain all the rights without any of the responsibilities.'[19]

The role of community

Within New Labour discourse, community performs the key function of inculcating the values of citizenship, social inclusion, and the social control of deviant behaviour. We can see this rationale underpinning the legislation. It is implicit in the Regulatory Impact Assessment in its discussion of the relationship between the Act and 'social attitudes', by which is meant that civil partnerships will strengthen communities and social cohesion. The deviant behaviour that is assumed to be in need of control through community is homophobia: 'The Government believes that the creation of a new legal status for same-sex couples would play an important role in increasing social acceptance of same-sex relationships, reducing homophobia and discrimination and building a safer and more inclusive society.'[20] By bringing their relationships into the public sphere – into the wider community – lesbians and gays can look forward to acceptance, inclusion and presumably full citizenship within that public space. The deviance of homophobia will (somehow) be controlled through the act of coming out as a couple. It is only through lesbians and gays entering the public sphere that homophobia is pushed out of that same sphere. Thus, gays are now required to leave the closet (rather than remain closeted) in order to advance the goal of social inclusion. While Conservative politicians once claimed that only by closeting themselves could lesbians and gays achieve acceptance and reduce homophobic violence, we now find a call to come out in order to achieve the same ends.

Family values

The importance of the family is pivotal as the ideological basis for the legislation. In particular, the family is cited for its central role in producing responsible, active new citizens, and as providing a counterbalance to rugged individualism and

---

17 *Ibid*, p 2.
18 DTI (2003), p 15.
19 *Ibid*, p 38.
20 DTI (2004), p 16.

atomisation. Furthermore, the family is largely indistinguishable from the import-ance of 'stable relationships', which have empirically *proven* benefits to indi-viduals and to society as a whole. These familial relationships are assumed to take a particular form based on a couple dyad, with or without children, and with little sense of extended familial relationships or alternative living arrangements. Although cohabitation is not a requirement of civil registration, there is an implicit assumption that registration and cohabitation will probably go hand in hand.

The benefits of this mode of living – assumed to be facilitated and enhanced by the Act – are far-reaching and, it is claimed, empirically grounded. These advantages of stable couplehood flow both to individuals and to society as a whole:

> The availability of civil partnership status would encourage stable relationships, which are an important asset to the community as a whole. It would reduce the likelihood of relationship breakdown, which has a proven link to both physical and mental ill health. As the Government said in its 1998 consultation document *Supporting Families*, 'Strong and stable families provide the best basis for raising children and for building strong and supportive communities'. Strengthening adult couple relationships not only benefits the couples themselves, but also other relatives they support and care for, and, in particular, their children as they grow up and become the couples, parents and carers of tomorrow.
>
> Stable relationships also benefit the economy. It is expected that civil partners would share their resources and support each other financially, reducing demand for support from the State and, overall, consuming fewer resources. Increased stability would help to reduce the burden on the State in terms of family breakdown, which cost the taxpayer an estimated £5 billion in 1999.[21]

Thus, the stable couple form is good for the individual, for the couple, and for society as a whole (both socially and economically). Living outside of that form is inefficient and costly, and the breakdown of the relationship form is both unhealthy and socially expensive. As a consequence, long-term stable relationships become the socially preferred option for government.

Consensus politics

The fifth aspect of New Labour ideology is a desire for consensus within One Nation, in which acceptance of multiculturalism and tolerance of 'difference' (within limits) prevails. This message is omnipresent in the material surrounding the legislation. Lesbians and gay men become understood as another constituency that needs to be managed. This is 'their' law and it is part of the government's 'gay agenda'. The Act is aimed at social inclusion of *this* group and certainly not at rectifying injustices more broadly. This is one of the ways in which the British approach can be distinguished from the French 'solution' of the *Pacte Civil de Solidarité* (PaCS).[22] The PaCS can be ideologically situated firmly within the

---

21 *Ibid.*
22 See, eg, Barlow and Probert (1999); Pratt (2002); Steiner (2000); Stychin (2003), ch 3.

French conception of republicanism and universality.[23] It is justified as a universal status to which all are equally entitled to participate on the basis of being members of the Republic. It is the antithesis of multiculturalism, which the French consistently describe as part of an 'Anglo-Saxon' mentality, which inevitably fragments social solidarity.[24]

By contrast, within the United Kingdom, the Civil Partnership Act is explicitly and specifically designed for one group – lesbians and gays – who are (problematically) constructed as another element within the multicultural mosaic. There is no expectation that the needs of other constituencies – such as platonic home sharers – can be solved by this legislation. These other groups must wait their turn.

The power of law

The final aspect of Third Way ideology is faith in law itself, and a belief in micromanagerialism through law. It is assumed throughout the documentation that surrounds the legislation that the availability of the legal status – as well as the difficulty in dissolution procedures for relationships – will encourage long-term, stable relationships. In this regard, law is thought to be a discourse of considerable power in shaping relationship forms, *granting to* lesbians and gays the very ability to live according to its norms. As well, law is assumed to be central in shaping social attitudes and, in particular, in reforming homophobia and encouraging tolerance and social inclusion.

Finally, perhaps less obviously, there is a message within the Act, I would argue, that the encouragement of the rights and responsibilities of civil partnership through law will provide a disincentive for 'irresponsible' behaviour. In the context of New Labour politics, irresponsibility seems to include promiscuous sex, relationship breakdown at will, and the selfishness of living alone (or perhaps even living with friends and acquaintances).[25] Thus, law is employed to achieve social policy ends that have been determined by government in advance based on empirical fact and science in order to help people to help themselves to lead richer lives.[26]

This analysis may provide an explanation for another stark difference between the Civil Partnership Act and the PaCS. The PaCS has been consistently characterised within French debate in terms of the values of autonomy and contract, as well as universality. It is claimed that the PaCS allows couples the freedom to enter and exit relationships with relative ease, with no expectation of sexual activity, or anything else particularly. It simply recognises a social reality, and law has a facilitative role in upholding that reality and in promoting the 'fraternity' of relationships. By contrast, the Civil Partnership Act is much more clearly a tool of social policy, and envisions relationships as possessing certain essential characteristics based upon a marriage model.

---

23 On French republicanism, see, eg, Favell (1998); Jennings (2000); Laborde (2001).
24 Stychin (2003), ch 3.
25 See generally Bell and Binnie (2000).
26 See McGhee (2003).

This provides an explanation for why the government chose not to adopt Lord Lester's approach – which bears some resemblance to the PaCS – of an alternative to the marriage model. The government desires nothing that could be perceived to undermine the value of the institution of marriage. Rather, the aim is to rectify a perceived unfairness within marriage for an equality-seeking constituency. This is grounded in an imagining of community in terms of groups and constituencies that need to be managed, rather than in terms of facilitating new ways of living for all.

Moreover, the adoption of a marriage model speaks to the relationship between law in its disciplinary mode, and law as enabling people to legally structure their lives as they see fit. Throughout New Labour's family discourse, we find great faith placed in an economically, socially, sexually disciplinary role for the institution of marriage: 'The government intends registered civil partnerships to be long-term, stable relationships, so there would be a formal court-based process for dissolution. The partner applying for the partnership to be dissolved would have to show that it had broken down irretrievably' and not simply that it felt right to end it.[27] Within this ideology of the family, there is no need for alternatives to marriage. Rather, there is a need for more encouragement to marry or to partner, particularly for the raising of children. As a consequence, there is absolutely no space within the parliamentary debates for any critique (feminist or otherwise) of the institution of marriage as a status. In these respects, the Act can be seen as deeply conservative and it is therefore not surprising that it received considerable support from within the Conservative Party. The message is inclusion rather than radical institutional change.

The irony, however, is that our current historical circumstances have been described in terms of the emergence of the 'postmodern family':

> the postmodern family represents no new normal family structure, but instead an irreversible condition of family diversity, choice, flux, and contest. The sequence and packaging of romance, courtship, love, marriage, sex, conception, gestation, parenthood and death are no longer predictable. Now that there is no consensus on the form a normal family should assume, every kind of family has become an alternative family.[28]

The Civil Partnership Act, in my view, attempts to flatten out that diversity into a recognisable and disciplinable legal guise. At the same moment, as Sasha Roseneil argues, 'the married, co-resident heterosexual couple with children no longer occupies the centre-ground of Western societies, and cannot be taken for granted as the basic unit in society'.[29] After all, only 23 per cent of households in the UK in 2000 were 'traditional' families.[30] Thus, the law seems to be attempting to bolster and recentre an institution in decline.

---

27 www.womenandequalityunit/lgbt/partnership.htm.
28 Stacey and Davenport (2002), p 356.
29 Roseneil (2002), p 34.
30 *Ibid.*

Queering partnership

For those who enjoy debating the politics of same-sex marriage, the Act provides a fertile source of material on which one can speculate whether the legal recognition of same-sex relationships is *assimilationist* (buying into an idealised heterosexual model of coupledom) or *transgressive* (challenging patriarchy by not conforming to a heterosexual, gendered model). However, the reason that this debate (certainly in the USA) appears interminable is precisely because it is unresolvable, in part because the regulation of sexual practice by the state is inevitably, as Davina Cooper has argued, 'complex, uneven and contested'.[31] It all depends upon the context, and there is no simple answer.

A more productive analytical approach is to look at the Act in terms of what it suggests regarding the role and function of family in law, such as the connection between relationship recognition and resources, and indeed, the public–private dichotomy itself.[32] Within the explanatory material and the debates, the role of relationships in promoting the privatisation of financial responsibility for care is apparent and explicit: 'The registration of a civil partnership involves both legal obligations as well as legal protections.'[33] Furthermore, one opts into this package of rights and responsibilities as a whole, with no possibility for 'pick and mix'. As a consequence, as the Financial Regulatory Impact Assessment makes clear, to repeat: 'Stable relationships also benefit the economy. It is expected that civil partners would share their resources and support each other financially, reducing demand for support from the State and, overall, consuming fewer resources.'[34] To receive the financial benefits of a marriage-like status, the responsibilities attach. The *quid pro quo* is explicit.

The most obvious example of this privatisation of responsibility is in the joint treatment for income-related benefits, which raises the possibility that registration will be financially detrimental for some couples. At this point, the government clearly recognises the problem of incentives. As the framework document makes clear:

> The Government proposes that civil partners should be treated as a single family unit for income-related benefit purposes. In addition, where appropriate unregistered cohabiting same-sex couples should also be assessed as a single family unit as is the case for unmarried cohabiting opposite-sex couples. The Government will ensure that this matter is handled sensitively ... Treating same-sex couples (where registered or unregistered), in the same way as opposite-sex couples (whether married or unmarried) in relation to income-related benefits is the best way to ensure fairness and ensures that a same-sex couple who wish to register a civil partnership would not be financially worse off than they would be if they chose not to register their partnership.[35]

Consequently, even if a couple choose not to 'buy into' the package of rights

---

31 Cooper (2002), p 232.
32 See, eg, Diduck (2001).
33 DTI (2003), p 38.
34 DTI (2004), p 16.
35 DTI (2003), p 23.

and responsibilities, they could be determined to be liable to treatment as a single family unit. Thus, the package of responsibilities is not quite as voluntary as is originally claimed, and this demonstrates the way in which cohabitation slides into an expectation of financial dependence, and how cohabitation and partnership are merged. As a consequence, we continue to have the spectre of the state determining when an unregistered couple is a couple for the purposes of financial responsibility, when they are flatmates, and when they are 'just friends' – categories that a queer critical analysis in large measure is designed to trouble.[36] Queer politics questions why partnerships which appear to mimic the most traditional aspects of heterosexual marriage are privileged while others are constructed as less deserving of recognition and, it appears, respect: 'A lesson of queer theory is that we should resist the tendency to trivialize, infantilize and subordinate relationships which are not clear parallels of the conventional, stable, long-term, cohabiting heterosexual couple.'[37] Ironically, the parliamentary debates underscore the extent to which Conservative opponents of the Civil Partnership Act – particularly in their claims that the Act is unfairly limited in its scope to same-sex couples – construct arguments that are remarkably similar to the queer critique.

To be clear, I am not suggesting that lesbian and gay people do not construct relationships of dependence. Some do, some don't, and those that do, do so in an infinite variety of ways. However, it may well be that lesbians and gay men, because of the lack of traditional family structures which were historically open to them, have had a greater opportunity for experimentation with varieties of interdependence in different forms and guises.[38] However, there is no recognition of this rich diversity in either the legislation itself, nor in the surrounding material, nor within parliamentary discourse. Certainly, the privatisation orthodoxy remains unchallenged. A similar argument could be made with respect to the ability to gain parental responsibility for children. Judith Stacey and Elizabeth Davenport, referring to the work of Martha Fineman, have suggested the abolition of the category of 'family' in law because of the way in which it 'renders women and children economically vulnerable to the vagaries of adult erotic and emotional attachments'.[39] The Civil Partnership Act aims to strengthen rather than to deprivilege that construct and does nothing about the dependence of children on the vagaries of emotional or sexual attachment within the family unit.

Focusing on the disciplinarity of the Civil Partnership Act can lead us, then, to ask about the possibilities that seem closed off under the guise of liberal social acceptance. What has been lost? The answer perhaps is to be found in the laboratories of social experimentation that have grown up through the exclusion from the legal and social family: that is, the variety of forms of relationship that demonstrate the limited imagination behind the Civil Partnership Act. A number of social commentators have argued that lesbian and gay lives can teach much about the variety of ways of living that, increasingly, we in the West can choose from as

---

36 See, eg, Bell and Binnie (2000); Butler (2002); Freeman (2002); Roseneil (2004).
37 Roseneil (2004), p 411.
38 *Ibid.*
39 Stacey and Davenport (2002), p 364. See also Fineman (2004), p 135; Diduck (2001).

we construct our lives.[40] At the precise same moment, the Civil Partnership Act falls back on a traditional conception of relationships, dependence, and privatisation. In this sense, the Act is an act of legal violence that delegitimises and shames that which it does not recognise: 'Crucially, cultural and legal recognition of same-sex couples would do nothing to enfranchise the relationships that have also been fundamental to queer life: friendships, cliques, tricks, sex buddies, ex-lovers, activist and support groups, and myriad others.'[41] As queers, we might advocate 'that institutions including the state would cease to make a singular form of love and sex into the matrix for its allocation of resources. What if one could have each of the things that marriage combines with a different person or small group? What if I could live with my mother, but still give my best friend hospital visitation rights and extend my health insurance benefits to my ex-lover?'[42] As Sasha Roseneil explains, these social practices are important in that they 'de-centre the primary significance that is commonly granted to sexual partnerships and the privileging of conjugal relationships, and suggests to us the importance of thinking beyond the conjugal imaginary'.[43]

Law seems unable, or perhaps just unwilling, to provide this kind of recognition – this thinking beyond – instead reducing the world to cohabiting partners with lives totally woven through with interdependence on the one hand, and 'just friends' on the other. But the complexity of queer life undermines that vision of privatised, familial domesticity, opening up new spaces for a post-familial world in which the provision of care is itself re-imagined beyond the partnership paradigm.

Concluding thoughts

In this chapter, I have interpreted the Civil Partnership Act as an act of legal discipline, but we might wonder whether we can also understand it in terms of opening up possibilities for resistance. While law may seek to close off possibilities – to discipline and to domesticate – we also have come to recognise the limits of law's discursive power. The power of law, after all, is always open to resistance, and the Civil Partnership Act is surely no exception.

It should be remembered that the Act does not completely mirror a marriage model. In at least two respects, it differs. Within the government commentary, there are interesting passages in which it is recognised that somehow (in quite an unexplained way) lesbian and gay relationships are different from marriage. First, and perhaps more obviously, there is no provision within the Act for voidability for lack of consummation:

> Consummation has a specific meaning within the context of heterosexual relation-ships and it would not be possible nor desirable to read this across to same-sex civil partnerships. The absence of any sexual activity within a relationship might be

---

40 See, eg, Giddens (1992); Weeks (2004).
41 Freeman (2002), p ix.
42 *Ibid.*
43 Roseneil (2004), p 411.

evidence of unreasonable behaviour leading to the irretrievable breakdown of a civil partnership, if brought about by the conduct of one of the parties. However, that would be a matter for individual dissolution proceedings.[44]

There is at least an implicit recognition here that same-sex partners may not sign up to quite the same comprehensive package of rights and duties expected within the institution of marriage.

Relatedly, there is no provision for automatic dissolution on the basis of adultery:

> Adultery has a specific meaning within the context of heterosexual relationships and it would not be possible nor desirable to read this across to same-sex civil partnerships. The conduct of a civil partner who is sexually unfaithful is as much a form of behaviour as any other. Whether it amounted to unreasonable behaviour on which dissolution proceedings could be grounded would be a matter for individual dissolution proceedings.[45]

Thus, while the supporters of the Act may imagine a particular target constituency – the cohabiting, sexually faithful and sexually active (with each other) same-sex couple – this disciplinary form of relationship is open to resistance within the terms of the Act itself. A couple need not be sharing a home to register as civil partners, nor need they be sexually active with each other, but they could be sexually active with others.

As the government makes clear, the Act is not aimed at home sharers, who may have a more financially intertwined life than same-sex civil partners. This leads to numerous questions: where does partnership end and home sharing begin? When is a couple a couple? When is it not? Is this a matter for individual autonomy or does it test the limits of the law, raising the issue of the authenticity of relationships? Might we witness the emergence of a new definition of a pretended family relationship? Perhaps, unwittingly, the Act allows us to bring to the public sphere new ways of living that might come to be recognised (or not) within the language of civil partnership.

Finally, there is surely no better place to engage in acts of resistance than at a wedding, with its abundance of rituals ripe for queer cultural appropriation. It should be remembered that the government itself recognises that there may be an important role for ceremony attached to civil registration. The importance rests not only in assisting the catering industry (an economic good), but presumably because the ceremony may further reinforce the seriousness of the occasion and strengthen the long-term emotional and financial commitment that civil partnership signifies.

We might ask what a 'queer wedding ceremony' might actually look like. First, a civil partnership ceremony is, perhaps by definition, a queer event, signifying both marriage and not-marriage at the same time. But, moreover, it may be at this ceremony – this strange heady mix of the public and the private – that the full fabulousness of queer existence can be displayed. After all, it is at the wedding

---

44 DTI (2003), p 36.
45 *Ibid*, p 35.

reception that the full panoply of mixed-up relationships in which queer lives are embedded can be exposed for public viewing. What could be more queer than that? Imagine the civil partners going off arm in arm with their respective different sexual partners, or back to their separate homes with their respective home sharers. The possibilities – the queer potential – are limited only by the queer imaginary, providing an extraordinary act of resistance (and a great party to boot). Just don't get me started on the gifts.

References

Auchmuty, R (2004) 'Same-sex marriage revived: Feminist critiques and legal strategy', 14 *Feminism & Psychology* 101

Barlow, A and Probert, R (1999) 'Reforming the rights of cohabitants: Lessons from across the channel', [1999] *Family Law* 477

Bell, D and Binnie, J (2000) *The Sexual Citizen: Queer Politics and Beyond*, Cambridge: Polity Press

Butler, J (2002) 'Is kinship always already heterosexual?' in Brown, W and Halley, J (eds) *Left Legalism/Left Critique*, Durham, NC: Duke University Press

Carabine, J and Monro, S (2004) 'Lesbian and gay politics and participation in New Labour's Britain', 11 *Social Politics* 312

Cooper, D (2002) 'Imagining the place of the state: Where governance and social power meet', in Richardson, D and Seidman, S (eds) *Handbook of Lesbian and Gay Studies*, London: Sage Publications

Department of Trade and Industry (DTI) (2003) *Responses to Civil Partnership: A Framework for the Legal Recognition of Same-Sex Couples*, London: DTI: www.womenandequalityunit.gov.uk/research/ pubn_2003.htm#civilpartnerships

DTI (2004) *Final Regulatory Impact Assessment (RIA): Civil Partnership*, London: DTI: www.dti.gov.uk/access/ria/index.html

Diduck, A (2001) 'A family by any other name ... or Starbucks comes to England', 28 *J of Law and Society* 290

Favell, A (1998) *Philosophies of Integration: Immigration and the Idea of Citizenship in France and Britain*, Basingstoke: Macmillan

Fineman, M (2004) *The Autonomy Myth: A Theory of Dependency*, New York: The New Press

Freeman, E (2002) *The Wedding Complex: Forms of Belonging in Modern American Culture*, Durham, NC: Duke University Press

Giddens, A (1992) *The Transformation of Intimacy*, Cambridge: Polity Press

Jennings, J (2000) 'Citizenship, republicanism and multiculturalism in contemporary France', 30 *British J of Political Science* 575

Laborde, C (2001) 'The culture(s) of the republic: Some contradictions in French republican thought', 29 *Political Theory* 716

McGhee, D (2003) 'Joined-up government, "community safety" and lesbian, gay, bisexual and transgender "active citizens" ', 23 *Critical Social Policy* 345

O'Donovan, K (1993) 'Marriage: A sacred or profane love machine?', 1 *Feminist Legal Studies* 75

Powell, M (2000) 'New Labour and the third way in the British welfare state: A new and distinctive approach?', 20 *Critical Social Policy* 39

Pratt, M (2002) 'Post-queer and beyond the PaCS: Contextualizing French responses to the civil solidarity pact', in Chedgzoy, K, Francis, E and Pratt, M (eds) *In a Queer Place: Sexuality and Belonging in British and European Context*, Aldershot: Ashgate

Rose, N (2000) 'Community, citizenship, and the third way', 43 *American Behavioral Scientist* 1395

Roseneil, S (2002) 'The heterosexual/homosexual binary: Past, present and future', in Richardson, D and Seidman, S (eds) *Handbook of Lesbian and Gay Studies*, London: Sage Publications

Roseneil, S (2004) 'Why we should care about friends: An argument for queering the care imaginary in social policy', 3 *Social Policy and Society* 409

Sevenhuijsen, S (2000) 'Caring in the third way: The relation between obligation, responsibility and care in third way discourse', 20 *Critical Social Policy* 5

Stacey, J and Davenport, E (2002) 'Queer families quack back', in Richardson, D and Seidman, S (eds) *Handbook of Lesbian and Gay Studies*, London: Sage Publications

Steiner, E (2000) 'The spirit of the new French registered partnership law: Promoting autonomy and pluralism or weakening marriage?', 12 *Child and Family Law Quarterly* 1

Stychin, C (2003) *Governing Sexuality: The Changing Politics of Citizenship and Law Reform*, Oxford: Hart Publishing

Weeks, J (2004) 'Same-sex partnerships', 14 *Feminism and Psychology* 158

Williams, F and Roseneil, S (2004) 'Public values of parenting and partnering: Voluntary organizations and welfare politics in New Labour's Britain', 11 *Social Politics* 181

Chapter 3
Shared Households: A New Paradigm for Thinking about the Reform of Domestic Property Relations

Anne Bottomley and Simone Wong

Introduction

When the Civil Partnership Act 2004 was being debated in Parliament, the chance was taken by a number of members of both Houses to raise, again, the plight of the female cohabitant who, at the end of a period of cohabitation (however lengthy) does not, unlike her married sister, have access to the divorce courts and thereby to property orders, which allow for the redistribution of property between the parties (however economically vulnerable she might be).[1]

What seems to have developed over the past few decades is a process of 'normalisation' of cohabitation, in that the 'reality' of cohabitation as an alternative to marriage status is now recognised as a choice made by an increasing number of people and as a choice which no longer, it seems, is marked with a significant social stigma.[2] As the legal and social consequences of being born outside of marriage as 'illegitimate' children have radically improved, so one of the major factors inhibiting cohabitation as a choice for those still of childbearing age has been removed. More and more benefits, as well as obligations, between domestic-sexual partners are now recognised and enforced (for instance, in relation to pension rights or the inheritance of tenancies), so that, at one level, it seems that we are now in a position to choose whether to marry our partners or not, without too many negative legal consequences. And yet . . . the figure of the economically vulnerable female cohabitant returns to haunt us. No family law text can now avoid addressing her position, and how easy it is to slip into contrasting her vulnerability with the seemingly more protected position of her married sister, especially given that the canon of family law remains firmly focused on marital status. And however 'normalised' and routine the role and position of the domestic-sexual partner in the media, readers of daily newspapers, or TV viewers, are treated on frequent occasions to stories of not only the wronged partner left after a long period of cohabitation and fighting for some (legal) recognition of what she contributed as well as what she lost, but also to stories of women who thought that after a period of cohabitation they would be treated as 'common-law wives' without any clear sense (except a vague idea that it would be an equivalent to marriage) of what benefit that might bring if such a thing did, in fact, exist in this country.[3] One is left with a sense that however 'normalised'

---

1   See, however, how strategic litigation can bring a case into the Family Division Bottomley, (1994a).
2   See, eg, Barlow and James (2004).
3   *Ibid.*

cohabitation has become, a significant number of women enter into it without either recognising the limitations of not having access to a property redistribution regime or taking the legal steps available to them to protect themselves (as far as it is possible) in relation to the shared use and ownership of property. The reasons for not taking steps to protect themselves need further investigation, but seem to range from believing in the myth of 'common-law marriage' and lack of basic legal information and advice through to believing in their men.[4]

It is not too surprising, within this frame, that the government has decided to invest a significant amount of money in an advertising campaign to let women know that there is one remaining significant disadvantage to not marrying – and that access to the divorce courts for economic orders makes a marriage certificate a valuable insurance policy.[5] But this is more than a warning to women not to slip without a lifebelt into the treacherous waters of cohabitation. The narrative of the plight of the economically vulnerable cohabitant underlines the function of marriage as a protective institution. Subtly, and very significantly, the government has made a fundamental choice here, even if only provisionally, about the location of marriage as a socio-legal institution. For the moment, the decision has been taken to keep marriage as an exclusive site of preferential significance. The centrality (and instability) of this decision is seen when we put together two trends in current socio-legal policy issues: dealing with the demands of same-sex couples for equal treatment and dealing with the figure of the economically vulnerable female cohabitant. It is therefore significant for this paper that we begin with the evocation of the latter in debates concerned with the recognition of the former.

The references to opposite-sex cohabitation in debates focused on same-sex registration seems, at first blush, rather strange. The Civil Partnership Bill was designed to meet the requirement of creating a status for same-sex couples which would satisfy the European Convention on Human Rights (ECHR) imperative for equal treatment and anti-discrimination on grounds of sexual orientation.[6] It remains questionable whether a status which is analogous to marriage, rather than opening marriage itself to same-sex partners, will be sufficient, but it is clearly the case that the British government believes the Civil Partnership Act to be sufficient and will defend it, if required, as meeting its obligations as it understands them.[7] To bring into debates on the Bill the issue of the unmarried opposite-sex cohabitant seems rather tangential; as the government reminded us with some frequency when addressing the issue of whether opposite-sex partners

---

4   *Ibid* and Bottomley (1994b). See also *Oxley v Hiscock* [2004] EWCA Civ 546, [2004] 3 All ER 703.

5   See the government's 'Living Together' campaign, which was launched on 15 July 2004. For further information, refer to the Department of Constitutional Affairs website at www.dca.gov.uk/family/cohabit.htm and www.advicenow.org.uk/.

6   See also Stychin, Chapter 2 in this volume.

7   *Hansard*, Commons, cols 177–8, 12 October 2004, Jacqui Smith. The government's view is that the Civil Partnership Act 2004 provides a ECHR-compliant secular approach to recognising stable and committed same-sex relationships and for such partners to receive the same rights and take on the same responsibilities as those who enter into a civil marriage, but without undermining (heterosexual) marriage.

should be allowed to register their partnership as an alternative to marriage, it was a question of having access to a status, and opposite-sex partners already had the choice of marriage. What more could they want? Why then raise the position of those who remained unmarried?

There were two important factors at work politically here: the first involved those who had been concerned about the position of vulnerable cohabitants for some time and were looking for opportunities to remind government and the public that their position had not been addressed (as far as they were concerned) with appropriate legislation which would allow for access to the courts and the redistribution of property.[8] The presence of this lobby is particularly interesting in that in most other European and Commonwealth jurisdictions such reform has now been enacted, either in terms of treating cohabitants after a period of time as if they were married (attributing marriage status and its consequences) or, more narrowly, allowing them access to the courts for the purposes of property redistribution. These jurisdictions met what were seen as the needs of the economically vulnerable female cohabitant by extending the attributes of marriage to include her before any of them dealt with the issue of same-sex partners and the recognition of their relationships, either through registration or through attribution based on sexual-domestic cohabitation. Within this schemata, the UK is not only well behind but also, in the thinking of less progressive lobbying groups, putting the wishes of same-sex couples before the needs of vulnerable women. Thus a concern with the plight of vulnerable cohabitants became blended with a different lobby, associated with the Christian right, to raise and use this figure along with other economically vulnerable figures of carers and sharers as part of a campaign to try and derail the Bill, which they saw as legitimating a status (and sexual practices) which would undermine the centrality of marriage.[9] As the Civil Partnership Bill reached the final stages of its passage, the government announced that the position of the economically vulnerable cohabitant would be referred to the Law Commission[10] and, in the publicity surrounding the passing of the Act, made clear that civil partnership was only an equivalent to marriage, therefore maintaining marriage as an exclusively heterosexual union.

Three themes continually play through the narratives of sharing domestic lives and property as they appear in these stories: marriage, female economic vulnerability and the imperative of equal treatment. As the narratives unfold, one fundamental subtext carries the momentum forward: the question of how far the benefits of marriage should be extended to others. Whether by attribution of status, piecemeal extensions, or by more limited recognition for certain purposes, for both same-sex and opposite-sex partners the issue has been, in this country, the initial breach of the exclusive benefits of marriage. Thus, in *Ghaidan v Mendoza*,

---

8 Especially the Law Society; see Law Society (2002).
9 See the advertisement placed by the Christian Institute in *The Times*, 9 November 2003. See also Stychin, Chapter 2 in this volume.
10 *Hansard*, Commons col 179, 12 October 2004, Jacqui Smith. The Property and Trusts Law section of the Law Commission has already looked, over a long period of time, into the question of property and home sharing but decided in 2002 not to make any recommendations for change. See Law Commission (2002). See now Law Commission (2006).

Buxton LJ, in the Court of Appeal, asked rhetorically why, having swallowed the camel (of recognising unmarried opposite-sex partners), the court should now 'strain at the gnat' (of recognising same-sex partners).[11]

And yet, although we can bring together the trajectory of cohabitation issues with the trajectory of same-sex partnership issues, in that they both meet on the question of the exclusive nature of marriage, 'on the ground' (in politics, texts and general conversations) they are too often presented as quite separate issues and, following the construction of the Civil Partnership Bill debates, sometimes as antithetical to each other, or at least in competition for government time. Indeed, the particular and contingent factors which structured the debates in 2002–4 have had, we would argue, a negative impact on discussions in this area. Whilst the two trajectories cross-cut each other but remain presented as separate issues promoted by different constituencies and interest groups, it makes it possible to utilise and present them as being in competition with each other, at least in terms of priorities for reform or academic funding.[12] What, crucially, has been effected is a closure of any space to think more carefully about 'why' certain categories of domestic relationships should be given a special status in law and with what effect. And, further, at the bases of both trajectories, the pattern of marriage and the powers of the court in relation to divorce and ancillary proceedings are presumed, without further examination, to be valuable socio-legal assets which should be extended to, shared with, other domestic partnerships.

In this chapter, we want to begin to open up a horizon beyond a preoccupation with immediate reform issues and to cross over and through the two trajectories, in order to see at what points they intersect and what issues this then raises. We will argue that both trajectories are couched in claims to be included into the existing legal regimes of recognition, and that the basic model, which is being stretched to include other categories, is a marriage model. This presumes that the marriage model is a satisfactory model, but it also, crucially for us, carries within this pattern of reasoning a presumption that, necessarily, extension to include other groups must be based on patterns of sameness or similarity – we will call this the 'logic of semblance'. The pattern of reasoning 'outwards' to allow for inclusion is interesting, in that we can trace shifts in what are seen to be the important characteristics of a relationship, which are rendered visible in order for the argument for inclusion to bite. But this then moves us to the core of our paper – it is our argument that if we become caught in the trajectory of 'semblance logic', we can only 'see' through a frame of reference that is constructed and constrained by patterns of similarity. It closes to view a very important debate for feminists, which is, simply: why should certain patterns of domestic relations be made visible in law and not others? The 'why' here is not addressed in terms of a larger debate about the many factors which have rendered some patterns visible to date, but rather addressed to feminists as a space to consider why we, as feminists,

---

11 [2002] EWCA Civ 1533; [2002] 4 All ER 1162, CA at 35.
12 Conversely, too much slippage between status issues and specific concerns with property often obfuscate the debate; such a slippage is all too easy, given the diversity of legislative programmes in the many jurisdictions which have tackled these issues.

would want certain patterns of relationships recognised for certain purposes. This is what we mean by a 'new paradigm': thinking not in terms of why the present privileges of law should be extended, but rather about what patterns we may want made visible in law.

Imagine, in order to bring our paradigm into operation, that we are in a utopian moment[13] when concerns about legal regulation are absent and we are simply dealing with an argument for why the law should recognise certain patterns of relationships for, in this case, the purposes of property re-adjustment. Our starting point begins very broadly – with the notion of a 'shared household', which is not defined by either sexual partners or familial relationships, but rather by a shared emotional economy. It is our contention that we should begin by envisaging such a household and then consider the kinds of patterns within such a household which might give rise to an argument for legal recognition (intervention) in relation to property issues. We could then move backwards into a discussion about whether certain patterns of relationships merit recognition either because of the high level of shared commitment which they exhibit or because of a pattern of social or economic vulnerability which arises as a consequence of the shared household arrangement. If we hold this paradigm as a place from which to view the existing patterns and calls for reform, we could begin by using this approach to highlight the ways in which patterns of semblance have played through at the moment in terms of 'what' is being recognised and 'how' it is being recognised. We can then return to the possibilities of thinking through our alternative category of 'shared households'.

Semblance logic: Sexual partnerships

On the one hand, we have the figure of the female cohabitant left economically vulnerable at the end of a period of cohabitation. On the other hand, we have the demand from many gay rights campaigners for access to marriage or to a marriage-like status. The momentum which directs the trajectory of each interest group is distinctive and presents very different agendas.

The figure of the female cohabitant is one based on a rhetoric of economic vulnerability lacking adequate protection in law. It draws its strength both from the generally recognised economic disadvantages of women and from the presumption that marital property regimes can and should, to some extent, redress this disadvantage at the end of a relationship. Therefore this concern can be met by focusing on a regime which allows access to marital property law without requiring a recognition of the relationship for other purposes.

Conversely, the concern with same-sex recognition is not based on economic vulnerability as a fundamental campaigning issue, but rather on a right to equal treatment by the recognition of a committed same-sex relationship through marriage status or an equivalent. Indeed, in the arguments put for such a recognition, concerns about inheritance tax and being recognised as the next of kin

---

13 The term and our usage of a 'utopian moment' is similar to the idea of 'liminal utopias' developed by Sargisson (1996).

were regularly raised by campaigners – not access to the courts for property redistribution purposes.

These two trajectories meet at one obvious point: when the argument is put for recognising cohabitants in order to protect the economically vulnerable woman, any proposals for reform will now have to meet the criteria of equality and non-discrimination and therefore be extended to cover same-sex partners as well. Therefore a concern to address one figure, the economically vulnerable woman, becomes hidden or enveloped in a gender-neutral form and also a 'sexuality-neutral' form.

There is a second pattern in play which takes us back to the Civil Partnership Act – the demand for equality is the momentum for establishing rights for same-sex couples, and the presumption for most people is that this is based on recognising sexual relationships. However, the Civil Partnership Act does not presume or require sexual practices of any form. Any same-sex partners can register under the Act, as long as they are of the same sex. The reasons are probably to do with a distaste in making visible and examining same-sex sexual practices; but the consequences of this distaste are interesting. What is hidden, or enveloped, is sexuality – it will probably be the case for most partners that it is their sexual partnership which forms the core of their commitment and which is being registered, but in law it is merely their commitment to each other which is being registered (unlike marriage, which presumes and requires both sexual practices and sexual fidelity).

Finally, a third pattern becomes visible: a concern that a fallback position is required for those who do not marry or register their relationship. It 'piggy-backs' on marriage and registration, in that it looks to similar relationships to extend some form of protection to them, but the question is then whether such protection should be limited to property re-adjustment or should carry with it a broader gamut of rights and responsibilities equivalent to those held by people who have married or registered.

The development of these patterns is particularly visible in Australian jurisdictions. For the purposes of the paper, we focus on three: the Property (Relationships) Act 1984 of New South Wales, the Domestic Relationships Act 1994 of the Australian Capital Territory and the Relationships Act 2003 of Tasmania.

Most Australian states began with addressing opposite-sex cohabitants only – for example, the *De Facto* Relationships Act New South Wales (1984) and Tasmania (1999) – and then amending or introducing statutes to extend protection to same-sex relationships[14] by redefining *de facto* couples. Most sub-national statutes have also retained a 'cohabitation requirement'.[15] For instance, s 4(1) of the Property (Relationships) Act 1984 redefines a *de facto* relationship as one

---

14 The *De Facto* Relationships Act (New South Wales) was amended and renamed the Property (Relationships) Act in 1999 so as to extend to both opposite- and same-sex *de facto* couples as well as carers, while Tasmania enacted the Relationships Act in 2003 to replace the earlier legislation and extend to both *de facto* couples and carers.

15 At present, only the Domestic Relationships Act and the Relationships Act do not impose a cohabitation requirement.

'between two adult persons: (a) who live together as a couple, and (b) who are not married to one another or related by family'.[16]

References to *de facto* partners 'living together as man and wife' are increasingly rare in the Australian legislation. The move from opposite sex to same sex, although clearly based on the image of a sexual partnership, becomes 'de-sexed' in an overt way by moving towards definitions based on what has become known as 'coupledom'.[17] If we are right in thinking that this is primarily due to an unwillingness to become caught in definitions of sexual practices (which lay at the root of marriage) when moving beyond opposite-sex sexual practices, then we have here an interesting doubling-back effect. A move from marriage into heterosexual practices remains defined by recognised sexual acts. Once, however, same-sex relationships are included, not only does the lack of sexual explicitness allow the heterosexual world not to have to think about what lesbians or gay men do in bed, but it also leads to a displacement of the centrality of sex for heterosexuals too, at least in the general structure of the legislation.[18]

For some advocates of gay rights focused on same-sex inclusion, the displacement of sexual practices is one which still fails fully to signal the fullness of their sexual partnership – an argument which is in full flow in both Canada and the United States, but seems, to date, more muted in Australia.[19] This may connect with the second trend, which is that the Australian developments have been based almost entirely on 'presumptive' rather than 'registration' regimes (the only exception being recent reforms in Tasmania). Therefore, the move from opposite sex to same sex has been more incremental, more subdued and more, we would argue, entwined with the original concerns with protecting the economically vulnerable rather than, *ab initio*, being focused on a claim to a right to marriage status or equivalent.

This decentring of sexual practices opens up a space for recognising 'relationships' which might not actually include a sexual element at all and allowing for other patterns of domestic interdependency which are not 'couple' based.[20] Parliamentary debates on the Civil Partnership Bill, and developments in Australian and Canadian jurisdictions, explored and extend this possibility. But, before we move on to examine this extension, we need to return to the boundary between marriage and other domestic statuses. At this point the question is: should any benefit be retained as exclusive to marriage?

---

16 *Cf* the previous definition found in s 3(1) of the *De Facto* Relationships Act (New South Wales), which reinforced the genders of the respective *de facto* partners twice in the definition.

17 See previously *De Facto* Relationships Act (New South Wales) s 3(1); *De Facto* Relationships Act (Tasmania), s 3; *cf* Property (Relationships) Act, s 4(1); Relationships Act, s 4(1).

18 The issue of the presence, or not, of a sexual relationship may well re-emerge at the level of guidelines given for, say, deciding whether a *de facto* relationship exists, or in the making of awards or dealing with case material.

19 Eg, Boyd and Young (2003); Millbank (1998); Millbank and Morgan (2001); Millbank and Sant (2000).

20 For a fuller discussion of this particular development in the Australian legislation and how this form of de-sexing is used to 'stretch' protection in relation to property matters to a wider range of relationships, see Wong (2004).

What is interesting in Australia is that earlier distinctions made between married couples and *de facto* relationships for the purposes of property adjustment orders have begun to erode, with some legislation like the Relationship Act and the Family Court Act 1997 of Western Australia demonstrating greater convergence between orthodox family law and *de facto* provisions. The Family Court Act is the most extreme example of wholesale transplantation of the marital provisions contained in the Family Law Act 1975 (Commonwealth) into legislation dealing with *de facto* relationships. As a result, the provisions applicable to married spouses on divorce are now equally applicable to opposite- and same-sex cohabitants in Western Australia.[21]

However, this convergence in terms of property redistribution retains the distinction of marriage (as an opt-in regime) and the broader rights and responsibilities carried within that status, leaving same-sex couples on a par with unmarried opposite-sex couples as in a type of informal arrangement, recognition of which would address possible economic vulnerability and allow for the question of equality to be played out rather than addressing status issues directly.

This suggests to us that the line drawn around marriage is permeable, both in the sense that it may be stretched to cover others for certain purposes, but also in the sense that it may be possible to 'let go' of certain characteristics which were once held as exclusive to those who had marriage status and therefore in part defined that status, whilst still maintaining (the possibility of) a site of 'marriage' as the 'real thing' as distinctive from the simulacra of marriage-types.

Semblance logic: Beyond sexuality

When the House of Lords first debated the Civil Partnership Bill, Lord Tebbit and others raised a simple question: why limit a right to register to same-sex (sexual) partners? If economic vulnerability arising from sharing a household – especially, for instance, when one party was caring for another – was an important factor[22] in extending legislative protection, why not allow others to register who defined their relationship not through sexual practices but through a shared commitment to live together and care for each other? There is a pattern here of Lord Tebbit *et al* trying to deflect the focus on equality onto a focus on economic vulnerability. The question was designed to derail the Bill, but it echoed concerns that had already been raised (for instance, inside the Law Society) with the economic vulnerability of domestic partners who lack a sexual nexus to their relationship. It is unfortunate that the figure of the 'spinster sister', developed by Lord Tebbit *et al*, caring for her (presumed) brother became reproduced in the gay press as the figure

---

21 The Relationships Act, on the other hand, does not go as far as the Family Court Act; the Tasmanian courts, for example, have more limited powers in relation to making maintenance orders. See Family Court Act s 205ZC and s 205ZD, which replicate Family Law Act (Cth) s 72 and s 75; *cf* Relationships Act s 46 and s 47.

22 This was rather disingenuous – it involved taking the focus away from equality arguments and placing it on economic vulnerability arguments.

being used to try and detract from the importance of the right to equal treatment for same-sex partners. It was argued, as it has been in Canada,[23] that this was a simple diversion from the main issue – and yet, it is our contention that it does raise some very significant issues.

Within the frame that Lord Tebbit was raising the issue, a clear attempt to wreck the Bill, it was also a badly muddle-headed approach if it were to be taken at all seriously. The Civil Partnership Act is about registration of relationships, not about the recognition of economic responsibilities for the sole purpose of property redistribution. It therefore raises issues of quite a different order to protecting the economically vulnerable through property redistribution. The narrower frame of property redistribution, and the more likely frame of presumptive regimes rather than registration, is the beginning of our examination of recent developments in Australia, which take seriously the issue of non-sexual domestic commitment.

The Domestic Relationships Act was the first Australian legislation to omit any reference to a sexual element to a relationship: it adopts a general definition, 'domestic relationship', defined as a relationship between two adult persons where 'one provides personal or financial commitment and support of a domestic nature for the material benefit of the other'.[24] No distinction (in the general frame of the Act) is made between *de facto* (sexual) relationships and others, for instance, care relationships. It further encompasses all these relationships regardless of whether the parties cohabit and 'share the same household' or not.[25] Since its introduction, no other sub-national legislation has adopted such a broad definition. While domestic relationships for the purposes of the Property (Relationships) Act and the Relationships Act cover *de facto* and other, especially 'care', relationships,[26] both statutes retain a distinction between the two types of relationships, thus affecting the convergence we mentioned above by distinguishing between rights given to *de facto* partners and lesser rights given to others. Both define a care relationship as one between two adult persons, whether or not related by family, where one or each of them provides the other with domestic support and personal care. A *de facto* relationship, however, is defined differently: s 4(1) of the Property (Relationships) Act defines the relationship as one between two adult persons who live together as a couple, while s 4(1) of the Relationships Act defines it as one between two adult persons who *have a relationship* as a couple. This means that cohabitation remains a prerequisite for inclusion of both opposite- and same-sex couples under the Property (Relationships) Act but not the Relationships Act.

The Relationships Act is significant in that it is the first Australian legislation to provide a dual (presumptive and registration) system for both *de facto* and care

---

23 Boyd and Young (2003).
24 Domestic Relationships Act, s 3(1).
25 Domestic Relationships Act, s 3(2)(a).
26 The qualifying relationships have been variously termed as 'domestic relationships' (as in the Property (Relationships) Act and the Domestic Relationships Act) and 'personal relationships' (in the Relationships Act). For the purposes of this chapter, 'domestic relationships' will be used, since it is the more commonly employed terminology.

relationships. The registration system under the Relationships Act is less formal than that provided in the Civil Partnership Act, which sets up registration and dissolution procedures for civil partnerships that mirror those of marriage and divorce. Under the Relationships Act, a deed of relationship may be registered upon satisfying the conditions specified in s 11,[27] and it may be revoked on the death or marriage of either party, or on the application of either or both of the parties to the Registrar, or on order of the court.[28] This means that an overtly non-sexual relationship may be registered. At one level, this seems very similar to the reforms recently introduced in Alberta (discussed later), which also allow for both *de facto* and other relationships to be registered, as well as introducing a fallback scheme of recognition. However, a crucial difference is that, whereas in Tasmania a line is drawn between *de facto* relationships and others, in Alberta they are treated in the same way and the line is drawn between married partners and others. What all these emerging patterns make clear is that extensions to cover others tend to include the drawing of lines around a central nexus of *either* marriage *or* sexual partnerships, although the unwillingness to speak of sexual practices tends to lead to a fudge which allows for slippage into non-sexual partners. This slippage has to be distinguished from the more definite moves made in some jurisdictions to extend protection to the economically vulnerable, especially carers, even if they meet at a point where a shift in focus to economic vulnerability allows detraction from the issue of equality for sexual partners.

In a sense, the recent Australian reforms not only extend to non-sexual care relationships; they also reveal an emerging trend, following the lead taken in the Domestic Relationships Act, of shifting the focus from the status of marriage and marriage-like relationships to one based instead on emotional and financial interdependence as indicators of a legally recognised relationship.

The significance of this shift is that it appears to move away from the 'sexual marriage model' as the starting point, thus providing access to the law to a wider range of relationships. However, if we are right in our arguments regarding the 'logic of semblance', this access may be questionable, as the focus of reform remains confined to relationships which are perceived by the law as 'signalling' commitment in a manner comparable to marriage.[29] In so doing, the law continues to look at bilateral relationships: that is, to forms of partnership between two persons capable of projecting the same signal to commitment and long-term

---

27 The parties (a) must be domiciled or ordinarily resident in Tasmania, (b) must not be married or a party to a deed of relationship, and (c) are in a significant or caring relationship. The second condition points to the need for exclusivity in order to qualify for registration of the relationship. Hence only parties in exclusive *de facto* or care relationships are permitted to register their relationship.

28 Relationships Act, s 15.

29 Rowthorn (2002), for instance, argues that marriage is traditionally seen as an institution for establishing a permanent and sexually exclusive union between a man and a woman. This 'signal' serves the threefold function of indicating: their commitment for an enduring relationship; their unavailability, sexually, to others; and the likely stability of the relationship. The application of signalling theory to marriage will have implications for any proposed reform of cohabitation and same-sex relationships, that reform calling for the recognition of such relationships would tend to favour a policy that ensures an effective signal of commitment and stability.

stability as marriage does. Further, the shift away from a sexual/marriage nexus is allowed for by re-engaging with a concern to protect the economically vulnerable, revealing a concern to strengthen ties of economic interdependency, again reproducing a marriage model or, rather, picking up on one of the major conventional functional aspects of a marriage model.

Reaching the limits of semblance logic: Constrained by bilateral thinking

Whilst we can see a stretching of the marriage model to include relationships not based within a sexual nexus, it is clear that the pattern of reform presumes a bilateral partnership.[30] If one aspect of the logic of semblance has been stretched to the point of loss, another (along with economic interdependency!) seems to remain. Why should we presume that a shared domestic household be limited to a bilateral relationship? A key question that arises is whether there is any rational and principled basis upon which the law should be limited to bilateral relationships. What potential is there in the existing Australian legislation, which exemplifies a broad approach, for moving beyond a bilateral model?

In defining all domestic relationships, whether between *de facto* partners or carers, the Property (Relationships) Act, Domestic Relationships Act and Relationships Act provide no scope for considering a wider range of home-sharing arrangements and confine the statutory regimes to bilateral relationships. The resolution of financial and property matters that arise on relationship termination have to be dealt with on a bilateral basis. This fails to acknowledge the existence of other more diverse and plural home-sharing arrangements. Cultural as well as economic factors (eg familial obligations to care for elderly parents; unmarried, divorced or widowed siblings living together or with parents; being priced out of the property market because of recent sharply increasing prices, etc) may variously affect people's reasons for sharing a household. Such arrangements clearly go beyond conventional bilateral models. For example, three unmarried friends or sisters, A, B and C, may decide to set up a shared household in the house belonging to C where they agree to provide each other with emotional and financial support and care. The application of the Property (Relationships) Act, the Domestic Relationships Act or the Relationships Act would create a complex web of legal relationships which would be unlikely to fit the emotional and financial map of the household. The presumptive system of each of the Australian statutes would permit the matrix of relationships shown in Table 3.1.

For the purposes of registration under the Relationships Act, if A and B were to register their care relationship, they would be unable to register their respective care relationships with C.[31] Likewise, if A and C were to register a deed of their relationship, they could not register their respective care relationships with B.

---

30 We could have employed the anthropological term 'dyad' but chose not to, given that this would have led us on to 'tryad'. However, what has been employed here is the use of 'stretch' as informed by the work of Strathern (1999).

31 Relationships Act, s 11(1)(b) and (2)(a).

Table 3.1 A, B and C: Possible relationships

	A	B	C
B	Care relationship	N/A	Care relationship
C	Care relationship	Care relationship	N/A

In addition, since A, B and C are simultaneously in other domestic relationships (see Table 3.1), none of them may register any of the relationships unless they opt for exclusivity.[32] Yet, under the presumptive system, the Act is silent on whether or not there is a similar bar on the creation of concurrent domestic relationships. Similarly, in both the Property (Relationships) Act and the Domestic Relationships Act there are no express provisions to indicate that the creation of concurrent domestic relationships is prohibited. Thus, it is arguable that the statutes envisage that possibility but only under the presumptive system.

This raises the issue of how competing claims by parties in concurrent domestic relationships are then to be dealt with. At present, little help can be gleaned from the case law, as almost all of the disputes that have gone to court have been between *de facto* partners. The experience in the Australian Capital Territory, for example, points to an under-use of the Domestic Relationships Act by other constituents, such as carers. Nor have there been cases involving claims by parties in concurrent relationships, which has probably not been helped by the way in which the statutes have been drafted to focus on claims being made on a bilateral rather than a multilateral basis.[33] That being the case, while classifying the various relationships may be simple enough, resolution of the respective and competing claims of A, B and C vis à vis one another on a bilateral basis is less likely to be so. For instance, in determining A's claim against C, there will be little, or no, consideration of the countervailing claims that B may make against either A's or C's assets. Some may argue that this is only fair, since A's entitlement, if any, should be determined by her contributions, financial and non-financial, towards C's care and support, and her claims against B or vice versa should thus be immaterial. This, however, is purist logic, as it ignores the interrelatedness of A's relationships with B and C respectively, which may not be easily disentangled and treated as separate and distinct, and abstracts A's contributions by taking them out of the context of the three-party home-sharing arrangement.

The matters which the respective sub-national courts may take into consideration in determining whether or not a property adjustment order should be made also vary. At one end of the spectrum is the Property (Relationships) Act, which, being the narrowest of the statutes, allows the New South Wales courts to take

---

32 See n 27 above; Relationships Act, s 15(1).

33 All three statutes refer to applications made in relation to the property of both parties or either of them, thus reinforcing the bilateral nature of the statutes. See Property (Relationships) Act, s 14(1); Domestic Relationships Act, s 15(1); Relationships Act, s 40(1).

into account only the contributions referred to in s 20(1)(a) and (b).[34] On the other hand, the Domestic Relationships Act and the Relationships Act allow the Australian Capital Territory and Tasmanian courts respectively to consider the financial needs and obligations of each party, and their respective responsibilities to support any other person as well as their future needs.[35] Reference to the parties' 'obligations' and 'responsibilities to support' may suggest that there is some scope for considering any countervailing claims which A, B and C may make as against each other when determining what order to make as between A and C. However, the extent to which such countervailing property adjustment orders will fall within the meaning of 'obligations' and 'responsibilities to support' is unclear. This leaves a gap in the existing Australian legislation about whether or not the courts can efficiently deal with multilateral relationships.

Our concern then is that the logic of semblance still holds one important aspect to it which dominates the pattern of extension and inclusion. All the legislative programmes which we have found have been based on the nexus of a 'couple': a bilateral partnership sharing a domestic economy. This may, in part, be derived from the prominence of the registration model based on a marriage model and that a presumptive model in effect generally 'piggy-backed' on this model. But it is this derivation, we shall argue, that has a major limiting effect on the development of a more progressive and informed debate as to why certain domestic arrangements should be recognised for property redistribution purposes.

A different paradigm: Beyond bilateral relationships

Should – or can – a model predicated upon bilateral relationships be extended beyond a bilateral model? To begin in the middle, the question of how far the model can, or should, be stretched is at issue only when we begin within the origins of the model itself, a presumption of the 'typical household' and the presumed patterns of economic vulnerability or shared commitment that are likely to arise. It is already clear that presumptions of a 'typical household' have to be modified to recognise a plethora of different living arrangements and the economic vulnerability or shared commitment which might arise from them. As the model is stretched to include other patterns of relationships, we have noted that it remains focused on bilateral partnerships, but that within this model what is exposed is a range of reasons for recognising such relationships – for instance, a focus on caring. If the reason for recognition is the factor of caring, quite simply, why should it be presumed that there is only one carer? If two sisters rather than one looked after their third sister, why should this model not be recognised? If four friends rather than two live together, why should this not be recognised?

A focus on caring takes us beyond sexual relationships and raises the issue of

---

34 These are financial and non-financial contributions made directly or indirectly towards the acquisition, improvement or conservation of any property, as well as domestic contributions for the welfare of the other party or the family constituted by the parties.

35 Domestic Relationships Act, s 19(2)(a)–(f); Relationships Act, s 47(2)(a)–(m).

protecting those who have become economically vulnerable through home sharing and especially through the role of caring. But this has now brought us full circle. The figure of the carer tends to be gendered – in both the speeches of Lord Tebbit *et al* and the responses from within the gay community (albeit echoing Lord Tebbit): 'she' is not merely daughter or sister but too often described as 'spinster sister'. It is the economically vulnerable woman who is being brought into play. Whilst we recognise that all too often it is, still, daughters and sisters who provide the function of caring in families, we are, necessarily, concerned with two aspects to this portrayal. First, to focus on a demand for law reform via this figure is to enter into the possibility that it is only active caring which will be 'rewarded' via property adjustment regimes, thus reproducing patterns of expected roles and economic dependency arising from them. The second is that it continues to construct a focus based on economic vulnerability. In fact, we think that a careful analysis of case law in both divorce cases and trusts cases shows that a crucial rethinking is already well under way, which we would want to support and sustain: economic vulnerability still plays a part, but there is now a focus on the partnership aspect of the relationship as a form of joint enterprise. Attention is paid to the vulnerability that may have arisen from that partnership, in combination with an increasing realisation that the assets of that partnership should be shared equitably.[36] Although structural economic factors will still construct this picture, increasingly the specific circumstances within which the partners constructed and acted out their partnership are now a focus.

If we take the starting point of a shared household, we can then ask whether certain types of relationship do require or merit a different level or form of recognition from others. We can, if you like, look backwards to marriage and other forms of sexual/emotional partnerships and investigate the factors which might argue for differential treatment, rather than saying: this looks like this, so, based on either an equality argument or a needs argument, it should be treated analogously.

Reaching the limits of semblance logic: Beyond economic vulnerability

What we are suggesting is that two concerns – equality and concern for economically vulnerable parties – have always been in play in the reform debates. It may seem that economic vulnerability is a very sound ground on which to argue for law reform, and that it is important, in particular for feminists, to keep open the figure of the economically vulnerable female. However, this focus limits us to looking at patterns of dependency, rather than looking beyond this to a more interactive pattern of shared commitment. It may well be that we already have the possibility of thinking of shared commitment as the key concern for intervention, as in the Australian material. All we are signalling here is that a shift to this focus is important, so that we will not continually be drawn back into looking for

---

36 See, eg, *White v White* [2001] 1 All ER 1; *Cowan v Cowan* [2001] 3 WLR 684; *Lambert v Lambert* [2003] Fam 103; *Miller v Miller; McFarlane v McFarlane* [2006] UKHL 24.

patterns of actual economic vulnerability as the factor for intervention. Thus, to support the trend in our own jurisdiction, in both family and trusts cases, in which the element of 'joint enterprise' is increasingly being recognised, is crucial, even if in the actual orders given, a pattern of recognising economic vulnerability continues, necessarily, to emerge. What we need to highlight is that we should not be tied to actual economic vulnerability but look rather to shared commitment as being the baseline. Hence our shared household model is not only a chance to think beyond bilateral relations but also a chance to think constructively about what it means to 'share'.

The underside of present legal reforms and of our own approach

We began, when we first introduced our notion of the 'shared household', with a reference to a 'utopian moment'. A point which has been made very succinctly by feminists in relation to the same-sex marriage debates is that it is all too easy to become constrained by the parameters which have been set by these debates into being forced to argue on one side or the other, when really one wants to begin in a very different place and to keep open the possibilities of thinking other futures, rather than being caught by the past. Butler, Boyd and Young, Stychin and Cooper, for example, all recognise the constraints and limitations of the way in which the debates are constructed within the political arena and how difficult it is to open spaces to think outside of these constraints.[37] All emphasise, Butler in particular, the closure which this can effect in trying to think more creatively about domestic relationships. But there is more than this – there is also the clear-sighted recognition that the way the debate is presently structured not only confirms present privileges in relation to marriage and marriage-like relationships, but also carries with it some very dangerous agendas. Writing with a particular concern with same-sex relationships, all are concerned that only certain types of relationship are likely to receive recognition at law – those which are most similar to a social marriage model (although through a process which de-signifies sexual practices and therefore sexuality) – and that this will therefore exclude more non-conformist practices. But all are also clear-sighted in their recognition that there are powerful forces in play that are not progressive, even if they work within, or alongside, a paradigm of equality discourse.

The first element of this is that a concern to include same-sex couples not only privileges marriage-like behaviour for same-sex partners, but also may be utilised to confirm a marriage model for opposite-sex couples and indeed the exclusivity of marriage status. In Alberta, for instance, the Adult Interdependent Relationships Act 2002 not only extends a registration model and a presumptive model to all and any 'interdependent partners'; the legislation also confirms, in its Preamble, the 'sanctity of marriage', referring to marriage as 'an institution that has traditional religious, social and cultural meaning', and draws a sharp distinction

---

37 Butler (2004); Boyd and Young (2003); Stychin, Chapter 2 in this volume; Cooper (2001; 2004).

between spouses and others.[38] Thus, at one legislative moment, it not only extends the marriage model but also limits 'real' marriage to heterosexual married couples. A similar move might be seen in this country in the decision to limit the Civil Partnership Act to same-sex partners, on the grounds that marriage law is available to opposite-sex partners, and a decision by the government to encourage the take-up of marriage status through an advertising campaign which focuses on the economic vulnerability of unmarried opposite-sex cohabitants. The Alberta legislation, further, does not mention same-sex partners, preferring to lose them in a more generalised package of 'interdependent relationships'. Not only is marriage preserved; same-sex recognition is also avoided. Further, as Boyd and Young[39] point out, this extension to a broad definition is clearly linked to a concern with the privatisation of welfare services – what is being accomplished here is a concern to make sure that domestic patterns are reinforced as patterns of economic dependency and where the function of caring should be either located or paid for.

Rights very rarely come without responsibilities, and 'recognition' is simply another word for 'intervention'. We referred in the introduction to one imperative on the government to reform the law in relation to same-sex couples being the equal treatment argument, but we are very aware of a second imperative: the increased use of economic modelling by academics and policy makers to inform reform proposals aimed at stabilising couples, families and households for the socio-economic good of the country. In the work of such academics as Bob Rowthorn,[40] in which legislative reform is simply one tool to achieve social ends, the use of 'family' law and the recognition of certain types of household is modelled in terms of whether it achieves its purposes: the stability of the unit. Within these terms, it is really not surprising that Tasmania has recognised care relationships or Alberta, interdependent relationships – it will help, it is thought, to stabilise them. The Civil Partnership Act, it is hoped, will stabilise male same-sex couples through patterns of regulation as much as through the privilege of recognition. In all cases, economic modelling can be used to suggest that being given a signal of commitment is a crucial factor – but it is important to remember that in both Tasmania and Alberta this signal is supplemented by the right of the state to recognise these relationships even when the partners have not chosen to utilise that signal.

Thus, it would be naïve of us not to recognise this element and further to recognise that the emergence of new patterns of household sharing may well 'require' forms of regulation which will be policed and achieved through recognition.

Social trends suggest that in this country we will see emerging households not corresponding to the 'typical type' as a response to such factors as the economics

---

38 The legislative process was a reaction to the Ontario Superior Court decision in *Halpern v Canada* [2001] 95 RFL (5th) 41. It included an amendment to the Preamble to the Marriage Act: 'Whereas marriage is the foundation of family and society, without which there would be neither civilization nor progress; Whereas marriage between a man and a woman has from time immemorial been firmly grounded in our legal tradition, one that is itself a reflection of long standing philosophical and religious traditions.' See Boyd and Young (2003) on Canadian reforms and also Butler (2004) and Cooper (2001; 2004) on wider issues.

39 Boyd and Young (2003). See also Stychin, Chapter 2 in this volume.

40 Rowthorn (2002).

of owner occupation, linked to the high cost of higher education and caring for the sick and elderly, etc. We are likely to see many more three-generation households, more friends buying together and often needing more than two members within the household economy – it may well become the case that these patterns will require, in policy terms, some recognition in order to stabilise them and minimise any economic fall-out if and when they break down in difficult circumstances.

The new paradigm: Shared households

We agree with Cooper when she argues that what we are witnessing is an extension of familial patterns into, and onto, other forms of social organisation: in this case, into the setting of households beyond those based on marriage. And we also agree with Boyd and Young that this form of disciplining not only confirms existing patterns of marriage and marriage-like relationships, but also is essentially a concern to stabilise units in order to vest the functions of economic responsibility and caring within the 'private' sphere. Any argument to extend these patterns can only seem, therefore, to be in these terms retrogressive or at least naïve. But we return to our 'utopian' moment and our model of the shared household.

Principally, we think that using the model of the shared household provides us with a frame through which we can more sharply consider present trends. The two most obvious trends we have indicated are the final constraints imposed by the 'logic of semblance': trends toward bilateral thinking and to a marriage-like model based either on the argument for equality or on the figure of the economically vulnerable party. Therefore, the only progressive move open to us, we think, is to argue beyond those limits: to argue from a perspective which takes the focus away from bilateral relationships and away from economic vulnerability.

It could be argued that in making this move we fail to address the specific issues of recognition of same-sex sexuality or a concern with actual economic vulnerability. But this does not need to be the case. By turning the argument around and taking a very broad approach we can, we think, leave open a series of questions about whether certain types of relationship should be given privileged recognition, or about when certain patterns of actual economic vulnerability should be recognised. The point is, however, not to presume that either sex or a fear of economic vulnerability is a sufficient reason for initial recognition. For instance, rather than presume that sexual partners are more economically entwined than others, we would like much more empirical work on whether this is the case. We would also like much more empirical work on whether, for instance, women are more willing to become economically vulnerable when 'protected' by the status of marriage or living in marriage-like relationships. We would also like much more consideration for why we, as feminists, might be willing to privilege sexual relationships over others and to keep open, as feminists, our concern with marriage and marriage-like models.[41]

---

41 See especially Boyd and Young (2003).

The strategy of thinking in terms of a shared household allows us to return to these questions; it also allows us to go further and to reclaim, in our utopian moment, the possibility of a much more diverse and fluid account of different forms of domestic sharing and to argue the validity of thinking, if not moving, beyond the limited accounts of domestic arrangements which have so constrained us in the past.

References

Barlow, A and James, G (2004) 'Regulating marriage and cohabitation in 21st century Britain', 67(2) *Modern Law Review* 143

Bottomley, A (1994a) 'Production of a text: *Hammond v Mitchell*', 2 *Feminist Legal Studies* 83

Bottomley, A (1994b) 'Language, gender and property relations: Songs of innocence and experience', in Eekelarr, J and Maclean, M (eds) *Families, Politics and the Law*, Oxford: Oxford University Press

Boyd, S and Young, C (2003) ' "From same-sex to no sex"?: Trends towards recognition of (same-sex) relationships in Canada', 1(3) *Seattle J for Social Justice* 757

Butler, J (2004) *Undoing Gender*, Abingdon: Routledge

Cooper, D (2001) 'Like counting stars?: Re-structuring equality and the socio-legal space of same-sex marriage', in Wintemute, R and Andenas, M (eds) *Legal Recognition of Same-Sex Partnerships: A Study of National, European and International Law*, Oxford: Hart Publishing

Cooper, D (2004) *Challenging Diversity*, Cambridge: Cambridge University Press

Graycar, R and Millbank, J (2000) 'The bride wore pink ... to the Property (Relationships) Legislation Amendment Act 1999: Relationships law reform in New South Wales', 17 *Canadian J of Family Law* 227

HC Deb, 12 October 2004 (425 c177–179)

HC Standing Committee D, 21 October 2004 (c050–051)

Law Commission (2002) *Sharing Homes: A Discussion Paper*, Law Commission (No 278)

Law Commission (2006) *Consultation Paper No 179: Cohabitation: The Financial Consequences of Relationship Breakdown*, London.

Law Society (2002) *Cohabitation: The Case for Clear Law: Proposals for Reform*

Millbank, J (1998) 'If Australian law opened its eyes to lesbian and gay families, what would it see?' *Australian J of Family Law*, AJFL LEXIS 10

Millbank, J and Morgan, W (2001) 'Let them eat cake and ice cream: Wanting something "more" from the relationship recognition menu', in Wintemute, R and Andenas, M (eds) *Legal Recognition of Same-Sex Partnerships: A Study of National, European and International Law*, Oxford: Hart Publishing

Millbank, J and Sant, K (2000) 'A bride in her everyday clothes: Same-sex relationship recognition in New South Wales', 22 *Sydney Law Review* 181

Rowthorn, R (2002) 'Marriage as a signal', in Dnes, A and Rowthorn, R (eds) *The Law and Economics of Marriage and Divorce*, Cambridge: Cambridge University Press

Sargisson, L (1996) *Contemporary Feminist Utopianism*, Abingdon: Routledge

Strathern, M (1999) *Property, Substance and Effect: Anthropological Essays on Persons and Things*, London: Athlone Press

Wong, S (2004) 'Property regimes for home-sharers: The Civil Partnership Bill and some Antipodean models', 26(4) *J of Social Welfare and Family Law* 361

Chapter 4
What Is a Parent?
Emily Jackson

Introduction

Because parents possess a bundle of important rights and duties, clear and unambiguous legal definitions of motherhood and fatherhood are self-evidently desirable. And yet the law has tended to assume that the existence of a parent–child link will simply be obvious. Whilst this may be true in the paradigm case of a child conceived through sexual intercourse and brought up by both her genetic progenitors, for an increasing number of children there may be genuine uncertainty about the identity of their parents. Reproductive technologies, as is commonly observed, have the potential to fragment our definitions of motherhood and fatherhood. Science, according to John Lawrence Hill, has 'distilled the various phases of procreation – coitus, conception and gestation – into their component parts, wreaking havoc on our prevailing conceptions of parenthood'.[1] Where there are a number of possible mothers and/or fathers, how should we choose between them in order to identify a child's *legal* parents?

At the outset, it is of course important to acknowledge that most children know who their parents are without any need to resort to a complex legal definition. This is because all of the various criteria that we associate with motherhood and fatherhood are crystallised in the same two people. Such parents fall within what we might refer to as the 'core of certainty' and represent what I intend to call the paradigm case. Outside of this core of certainty lies a 'penumbra of uncertainty' in which the normal incidents of parenthood are more widely distributed. Here, we may have more than one woman who has a plausible reason to believe that she is a particular child's mother. For example, following egg or embryo donation, or IVF surrogacy, a woman gives birth to a child to whom she is not genetically related. Two women might then claim to be the *biological* mother of the same child. In such cases, the identity of the child's legal mother is not obvious. Rather, outside of the paradigm case, we must *decide* which of the various candidates has the better claim to be considered the child's legal mother.

Yet framing the question in this way uncritically accepts what I believe to be the law's principal stumbling block, namely its assumption that a child can have only two legal parents: one mother and one father. Conventionally, legal parenthood has been an indivisible and exclusive status: either you are a child's mother or father, or you are not.[2] Provided that one woman is recognised as a child's legal mother, no other woman can have her 'motherhood' of the same child acknowledged simultaneously. This is, I shall argue, unnecessarily confusing for children, who may find it harder to understand that one of their 'mothers' is a legal stranger

---

1   Hill (1991).
2   Bartlett (1984), p 879. See also Jones, Chapter 5 in this volume.

than they would living with the reality that two women stand in a maternal relationship towards them.

In this chapter, I propose to examine what we mean by the word 'parent', both in the paradigm case and within the penumbra of uncertainty. A number of different criteria ground our definition of parenthood, and while in the paradigm case these are all present within the same two people, within the penumbra of uncertainty they may be split between different individuals. Because the law has been stymied by the principle of parental exclusivity, its response to the splitting of the normal incidents of parenthood has been to try to identify a hierarchy of criteria which will result in one putative parent's claim trumping the others. In so doing, it has become spectacularly confused and confusing, not least because different hierarchies operate in different circumstances. So, for instance, the intention to become a parent will sometimes trump genetic relatedness, while at other times, the genetic link is decisive. I will suggest that the quest to identify one mother and one father within the penumbra of uncertainty has been a profoundly misguided enterprise. If instead we were to acknowledge the reality that some children have more than one mother and/or father, I think that we might be able to reach a solution that would have both practical and symbolic advantages for children and their parents.

In addition to the existing technological and social re-ordering of family life, new pressures on the legal meaning of parenthood can be foreseen. It seems that within a few years it will be possible to create gametes artificially, the most likely source being stem cell lines which have been extracted from human embryos. This will mean that same-sex couples will be able to have children who are genetically related to both of them. It is already possible to create what are known as parthonotes: that is, eggs which appear to begin the process of cell division without having been fertilised. Parthenogenesis – from the Greek for 'virgin birth' – might involve a child having only one biological parent. If human reproductive cloning becomes a reality, there will inevitably be considerable confusion over the resulting child's parentage. Is the DNA source the child's sole parent? Alternatively, is the woman whose denucleated egg was used also a biological parent? And what about the woman who gestates the pregnancy? Could such children therefore plausibly have three mothers?

My first task in this chapter is to offer some criticism of the way in which the law has tended to approach the question of the identification of parents. I intend to argue that the law has become hopelessly muddled and incoherent, and that it is time to rethink some of the assumptions which have traditionally underpinned the legal status of parenthood.

The paradigm case: What are the defining features of parenthood?

There are a number of ways in which we might identify a child's parents. For mothers, these are currently: (1) giving birth; (2) contributing the egg; and (3) intending to raise the child. For fathers, they are: (1) contributing the sperm; (2) intending to raise the child; (3) being married to the child's mother; and

(4) being registered on the child's birth certificate.[3] Almost all mothers satisfy all three criteria, and many – although by no means all – fathers will fulfil all four. Where each of the three defining features of motherhood vest in one woman, and all four defining features of fatherhood vest in one man, we have an example of the paradigm case, in which the parenthood of a child is entirely straightforward. Of course, that child might subsequently be adopted, which would result in the separation of, *inter alia*, the intention to raise the child and genetic relatedness. Given the availability of legal adoption, even within the paradigm case, legal parenthood is necessarily potentially impermanent.

Nevertheless, where a man and a woman conceive a child sexually, within marriage, whom they intend to raise, we can unproblematically accept that they are that child's parents. Some parents who differ only marginally from this paradigm case will also very obviously be a child's parents. An unmarried father, for example, who is registered on the birth certificate, genetically related to his child and intends to raise her is unquestionably that child's father.

But what if we move slightly further away from the paradigm case. What if, for example, a child is conceived using donated sperm? Here, we might have a man who intends to raise the child; is married to the child's mother; and is registered on the birth certificate, and *another* man whose sperm was used to fertilise the mother's egg. Who is the 'father' of this child? Following a surrogacy arrangement, we will have a woman who intends to raise the child and who may have contributed the egg, and *another* woman who gestated the pregnancy and gave birth. Which woman is this child's mother? Because the principle of parental exclusivity insists that one mother and one father must be singled out, the conventional approach to answering these questions has been to try to work out which of the features that we normally associate with parenthood should be decisive. While this might be relatively straightforward if a universally applicable hierarchy could be devised through which one factor – such as the genetic link – always took priority, as we see in the next sections, the law has instead used different tests in different circumstances, resulting in an extraordinarily incoherent approach to the identification of parents.

The current law

Paternity

At common law, the husband of a married woman is presumed to be the genetic father of any child that she bears (*pater est quem nuptiae demonstrant*), and is therefore automatically treated as the child's legal father from birth. This presumption was, however, always rebuttable by proof that the mother's husband could not be the child's genetic father. Before blood tests were available, the sort of evidence that might displace the presumption would be that the husband was sterile or impotent, or that he had been *extra quatuor maria* (beyond the four seas

---

3   Births and Deaths Registration Act 1953, s 34(2).

of England) at the time of conception. While the presumption of paternity within marriage usually simply confirms the genetic father's identity, at times it results in a legal fiction. A child's mother and 'father' may both know that another man is the true biological father, but the presumption enables them to conceal the extra-marital conception. This common-law rule works, therefore, not to promote truth about a child's genetic origins, but rather to safeguard the traditional family unit.

Since the 1940s, blood tests have been able to assist in identifying the child's genetic father. Until fairly recently, blood tests could only rule out a man's paternity. A man who shared the child's blood group might be her father, but so might any other man with the same blood group. Only if a man's blood group revealed that he could not have fathered this child was decisive evidence available that he could not be her father. Over the last twenty years, DNA fingerprinting has enabled paternity to be proved with a degree of accuracy which now comes very close to complete certainty. Under s 20(1) of the Family Law Reform Act 1969, as amended, the court may 'give a direction for the use of scientific tests to ascertain whether such tests show that a party to the proceedings is or is not the father or mother of that person'. Inferences are drawn from a putative parent's refusal to be tested.[4] The purpose of a s 20 direction is therefore now to *establish* paternity, rather than to exclude it as a possibility.[5] In the past, the courts were sometimes persuaded that blood tests to establish the child's paternity might not be in her best interests, because the results might disrupt the stability of the child's family unit.[6] More recently, the courts have increasingly insisted that there could be very few cases where it would be in the child's best interests for the truth about her paternity to be suppressed.[7]

Genetics as the test for paternity is, however, routinely trumped by intention following donor insemination. When treatment is provided in licensed clinics, the sperm donor will have signed a consent form agreeing to waive his right to be recognised as the father of any children conceived using his gametes. Donation is then conditional upon the donor's clearly expressed intention *not* to become a father. If the woman being treated in a licensed clinic with donated sperm is married, the presumption is that her husband has agreed to be treated as the father of any child that may be born as a result of the treatment.[8] He can avoid being recognised as the child's legal father only if he can establish that he did *not* consent to the treatment received by his wife. If the woman is unmarried, her heterosexual partner will be the legal father of any child that may be born, provided that the couple were treated 'together'. On a literal interpretation, this latter provision is misleading because the male partner will not have received any treatment himself. Instead, what has to be demonstrated is that 'the doctor

---

4   Family Law Reform Act 1969, s 23(1); *In re A (A Minor) (Paternity: Refusal of Blood Test)* [1994] 2 FLR 463.
5   *Re H (A Minor) (Blood Tests: Parental Rights)* [1996] 3 WLR 505; *Re J (A Minor) (Wardship)* [1988] 1 FLR 65.
6   *Re F (A Minor) (Blood Tests: Parental Rights)* [1993] Fam 314.
7   *Re H and A (Paternity: Blood Tests)* [2002] EWCA Civ 383, [2002] 1 FLR 1145.
8   Human Fertilisation and Embryology Act 1990, s 28(2).

was responding to a request for . . . treatment made by the woman and the man as a couple'.[9]

Despite the statute's rather ambiguous wording, the purpose of this rule is clear: if the clinic is aware of the unmarried man's *intention* to become the father of any child born following treatment, the law will recognise him as the child's legal father. Because it is routine to demand that both husbands and unmarried male partners sign consent forms agreeing to be treated as the father of any child who might be born following treatment, there is usually decisive proof of intent. As a result, disputes about paternity following fertility treatment are uncommon, although, as demonstrated by *Re D (a child)*[10] and *Leeds Teaching Hospital NHS Trust v A*,[11] not unprecedented.

In *Re D (a child)*, a woman sought treatment with donated sperm after she and her partner, with whom she had previously undergone treatment, had split up. She did not tell the clinic that the relationship was over, and as a result the clinic relied upon the earlier consent forms, which had been signed by her and her ex-partner. The House of Lords held that whether a couple were being 'treated together' under s 28(3) should be judged at the time of embryo transfer or insemination, and not when the couple were first accepted for treatment. Hence, in this case, the ex-partner was not being 'treated together' with the child's mother at the relevant time, so he could not be recognised as the child's legal father. A different sort of dispute arose in *Leeds Teaching Hospital NHS Trust v A*, where Mr B's sperm was used to fertilise Mrs A's eggs by mistake. Mr A had consented to the use of his own sperm to fertilise his wife's eggs, and not to the treatment which his wife actually received, and he was therefore unable to acquire paternity under s 28(2). So, while intention can trump genetic fatherhood under the 1990 Act, this will be possible only if the facts fit squarely within the terms of s 28.

Intention is also only able to trump genetic fatherhood if the sperm has been provided in accordance with the consent requirements laid out in both the Human Fertilisation and Embryology Act 1990[12] and the Human Fertilisation and Embryology Authority's Code of Practice.[13] If these conditions are not met – for example, if a woman inseminates herself at home with sperm obtained through a private arrangement or purchased over the internet – genetic paternity takes priority over intention. Should this woman be married, her husband will be treated as the child's father, although this common-law presumption might be trumped by genetic tests which identify the sperm donor. If she registers a different man – her unmarried partner, for example – as the child's father, there is again a presumption of his paternity which could be rebutted by genetic evidence. Once identified, the sperm donor would be under a duty to maintain his child throughout minority.

Following a surrogacy arrangement with a married woman, the child's legal father will initially be the surrogate mother's husband, who is neither the intended

---

9 *U v W (Attorney General Intervening)* [1998] Fam 29, *per* Wilson J, p 40.
10 [2005] UKHL 33, [2005] 2 FCR 223
11 [2003] EWHC 259, [2003] 1 FLR 1091.
12 Schedule 3.
13 Human Fertilisation and Embriology Authority (HFEA) (2004), Part 6.

nor the genetic father, but acquires his paternity through the common-law presumption of legitimacy within marriage. This might subsequently be rebutted by genetic tests that reveal him to be unrelated to the child. And fatherhood can be formally transferred through either adoption or the special procedure introduced by s 30 of the Human Fertilisation and Embryology Act 1990. Nevertheless, from the moment of the child's birth, a man who did not instigate the child's conception, who is not genetically related to the child, and who usually has no desire or intention to play any part in the child's life will have the right to take decisions about her upbringing, and will be obliged to maintain the child. Conversely, the genetic and intended father will initially bear no responsibility for 'his' child.

Because neither adoption nor the s 30 procedure is straightforward, not all surrogacy arrangements culminate in the formal transfer of legal parenthood. For obvious reasons, it is impossible to tell how many unofficial transfers of children take place each year. Worryingly, however, the Brazier Report concluded that 'a substantial proportion of commissioning couples are failing to apply to the courts to become the legal parents of the child'.[14] In such situations, the surrogate mother's husband (if she has one) remains the legal father, and the man who is bringing up the child may be a legal stranger to 'his' child.

A compelling illustration of the illogicality of the UK's rules on paternity following surrogacy is provided by applying them to the infamous American case *In re Marriage of Buzzanca*.[15] In his divorce petition, John Buzzanca asserted that his marriage to Luanne Buzzanca had been childless. Luanne Buzzanca responded by claiming that a surrogate mother (SM) was expecting the couple's first child. Jaycee Buzzanca, who was born six days later, had been conceived using sperm and eggs from anonymous donors (let us call the sperm donor SD and the egg donor ED). The surrogate and her husband (SM and SH) did not seek to become Jaycee's parents. The question for the court was a complex one. Out of the three plausible candidates for fatherhood (John Buzzanca, SD, SH) and the three possible mothers (Luanne Buzzanca, ED and SM), who were Jaycee's legal parents?

At first instance, the trial judge reached the rather surprising conclusion that, despite this surfeit of possible mothers and fathers, none could be considered Jaycee's legal parents and Jaycee must be judged to be a legal orphan. This was reversed on appeal, when the court held that because Mr and Mrs Buzzanca had jointly initiated Jaycee's conception, they were her legal parents and they were both therefore under a duty to contribute to her support. As a matter of justice, this seems right. John Buzzanca had deliberately instigated Jaycee's unconventional conception, and it would seem iniquitous for the law to allow him to shrug off any legal responsibility for the resulting child. John Buzzanca is Jaycee's father because without the Buzzancas' decision to become parents through this bizarre arrangement, Jaycee would never have been born. Identifying the surrogate mother's husband as Jaycee's father (as English law would have

---

14 Brazier *et al* (1998), para 5.7.
15 72 Cal Rptr 2d 280 (Ct App 1998), review denied, No S069696, 1998 Cal LEXIS 3830 (June 10, 1998).

done) would absolve John Buzzanca of his responsibility for the life he deliberately created, and instead pass legal responsibility for Jaycee's well-being for the next 18 years to a man who was not genetically related to her and who never intended or wanted to become her father.

So we can see that, outside of the paradigm case, the test for legal fatherhood varies according to the circumstances. A *genetic* link will usually – though not always – determine fatherhood in cases of disputed paternity, where the mother was having sexual intercourse with two men at the time of conception. If a child is conceived using donated sperm, *intention* will trump the genetic link, provided that insemination took place in a licensed clinic. But if the sperm donation was accomplished informally, *genetic* relatedness will be decisive. Following a surrogate birth, it is the man's *relationship* with the child's mother that normally determines the identity of the child's father. Given this hotchpotch of competing presumptions and hierarchies, the identity of a child's legal father is patently not a self-evident question of fact.

Maternity

In English law, while motherhood may subsequently be transferred by adoption or the s 30 procedure, *ab initio* a child's legal mother will always be the woman who gave birth to her. Although now also given statutory effect,[16] this common-law rule derives from the maxim *mater est quam gestatio demonstrat* (by gestation, the mother is demonstrated). Or, in the words of Lord Simon in the *Ampthill Peerage* case, maternity is 'proved demonstrably by parturition'.[17] Yet we immediately have a source of confusion here. Is it gestation itself that is decisive, or does gestation merely *demonstrate* or offer proof that the woman who gives birth is the *genetic* mother of the child? So, while usually assumed to mean that legal motherhood always vests in the gestational mother, an alternative interpretation of this common-law rule could be that the test for motherhood is in fact genetic relatedness, rather than gestation. Until the development of *in vitro* fertilisation techniques, gestation simply constituted irrefutable evidence of the decisive genetic link.

The adoption of a universal gestational test for maternity is usually, of course, unproblematic. Its principal defect is its application to undisputed surrogacy arrangements, when the rule will vest maternal status in a woman who never intended to be the child's mother. Because most surrogate mothers do want to hand over the baby after birth, the practical consequence of the universal gestation-based test is that the child is born into a legal limbo which will continue until parental status and responsibility are formally transferred via judicial proceedings. And, as noted earlier, since no formal transfer will ever take place in a 'substantial proportion' of cases, this legal limbo may continue throughout the child's life. This sort of uncertainty, even if relatively short-lived, is clearly not in the best interests of the child. In the absence of a dispute, it would therefore

16 Human Fertilisation and Embryology Act 1990, s 27.
17 [1977] AC 547, p 577.

seem sensible for intention to be decisive. In the handful of cases where there is a disagreement over the child's parentage, some mechanism to resolve the dispute must be found. This could consist in a default test (gestation or intention, for example), or in some sort of 'best interests' assessment.

In England, depending upon the context, a variety of tests can be employed in order to identify a child's legal father. In sharp contrast, the definition of 'mother' is rigidly inflexible and inattentive to the different contexts in which children are conceived. Of course, women's gestational capacity is clearly a material difference between the sexes, and therefore adopting differential tests for motherhood and fatherhood is not presumptively discriminatory. But if we think about some of the reasons for gestational priority, a powerful argument against differential treatment of men and women emerges. Both men and women can, via gamete donation, voluntarily surrender their parental status prior to a child's conception. But the gestational mother's decision to relinquish her parental status will be ineffective until at least six weeks after her child's birth.[18] The only plausible explanation for the difference is that women are assumed to be incapable of making this decision before and during pregnancy, and within the first six weeks of the child's life. There is, in short, a danger that women might change their minds, and that their subsequent regret would be intolerable, which, according to Marjorie Shultz, reinforces 'the sexist stereotype that women are ruled by unpredictable emotion'.[19] For men and non-pregnant women, parenthood can be acquired and transferred by clear expressions of intent on the part of the social and genetic parents. For gestating women, 'biology is still destiny'.[20]

The advantages and disadvantages of parental exclusivity

By restricting the number of parents a child may have to one mother and one father, the law is unable adequately to accommodate increasingly complex reproductive arrangements. Children born following surrogacy arrangements, or children who have been adopted, have *two* mothers. When donated gametes are used, the genetic parent and the social parent are different people, but both are in different ways *parents*. One is a parent, in the sense that they do the job of parenting, whereas the other is the provider of half of the child's DNA. Perhaps part of the problem is that the word 'parent' itself has a number of different meanings. As a noun, it could apply to both genetic and social parents, but as a verb, it refers only to the work involved in bringing up a child.

Why has the law continued to rely upon an exclusive model of parenthood despite the technical and social fragmentation of the normal incidents of maternity and paternity? The obvious answer is itself revealing. If a child has only one mother and one father, we can be certain about who possesses the various rights and obligations that attach to the status of being a parent. Were we to recognise

---

18 See O'Donovan and Marshall, Chapter 6 in this volume.
19 Shultz (1990), p 352.
20 *Ibid*, p 394.

multiple parents, we would have to decide which 'parents' should be obliged to maintain the child; which should be the primary caretakers; and so on. Parental exclusivity thus appears to have the merit of certainty. Yet this superficially appealing explanation in fact presupposes what it seeks to prove.

Consider, for example, our assumption that – barring serious ill treatment – the child's parents have the right to be the primary caretakers throughout childhood. As Lord Templeman famously explained in *Re KD (A Minor) (Ward: Termination of Access)*: 'The best person to bring up a child is the natural parent. It matters not whether the parent is wise or foolish, rich or poor, educated or illiterate, provided the child's moral and physical health are not endangered.'[21] If we are genuinely uncertain about who a child's parents might be, then their 'right' to be recognised as the child's primary caretakers is essentially meaningless. It will point only to a number of candidates who cannot logically *all* have the *prima facie* right to care for the same child. Where there is more than one woman with a credible claim to be considered the child's mother, there is no escaping the need to *decide* which woman should acquire the right to be considered the child's principal caretaker. To say that this right vests with the child's mother simply begs the question. With baffling circularity, then, in trying to decide between a number of possible mothers and/or fathers, the law in fact assumes that every child will have two (and no more than two) clearly identifiable parents.

The identification of parents is conventionally believed to be a question of fact rather than judgment, and so the test we employ in order to identify a child's mother and father is supposed simply to locate the truth about the child's origins. The problem, of course, is that there may be no obvious 'truth' to be discovered. Following egg donation, it is not necessarily self-evident whether the genetic mother or the woman who gives birth is properly described as the child's mother. If parenthood is not a fact waiting to be discovered, we are going to have to make some decisions about the relative importance of various different aspects of motherhood and fatherhood. But introducing this element of *choice* into the identification of parents is profoundly counter-intuitive, and, as a result, it is probably unsurprising that the law has been reluctant to abandon the idea of a clear, factual test for parenthood. Judge De Meyer advocated just such a simple, but ultimately circular, definition of fatherhood in the judgment of the European Court of Human Rights in *X, Y and Z v United Kingdom*[22] when he said that 'it is self-evident that a person who is manifestly not the father of a child has no right to be recognised as the father',[23] as if, as Andrew Bainham has pointed out, 'we all know a father when we see one'.[24] Illogically, then, when identifying a child's parents, we 'implicitly appeal to some simple preanalytic concept of parenthood',[25] when the reason why we need this definition in the first place is that genuine uncertainty exists. And of course, we can only be uncertain about who

---

21 [1988] AC 806, p 812.
22 (1997) 24 EHRR 143.
23 *Ibid*, p 175.
24 Bainham (1999), p 25.
25 Hill (1991), p 360.

should be considered a child's parents if our concept of parenthood is much more fluid than we may have supposed.

The decision about who should have the *prima facie* right and duty to look after a particular child is no less a decision just because we present it as a question of fact (ie, who *is* the child's mother?) rather than judgment (ie, who do we think *deserves* to have their parental claim given priority?). Admittedly, the law does not engage in a case-by-case determination of parenthood in order to allocate it to the persons who are best able to meet a particular child's needs. But making intention – rather than the genetic link – the factor which determines the paternity of children born following sperm donation is nonetheless a *decision* rather than a straightforward question of fact. Preferring to give surrogate mothers and their husbands first refusal on the rights and obligations of parenthood is a *choice* which is obscured by the law's insistence that gestation – as opposed to genetic relatedness or the intention to raise the child – is the defining feature of motherhood.

In addition to its obfuscatory function, the 'all or nothing' quality of parental status creates a further problem. Where the normal incidents of parenthood are distributed more widely than in the paradigm case, but the law has identified just one mother and one father, what is the status of the non-parents who nevertheless possess one or more of the normal incidents of parenthood? Because the law admits no middle ground here, such people are *prima facie* legal strangers to the child. So – to take IVF surrogacy as an example – the gestational mother is *the* legal mother, and the genetic and intended 'mother' is, in fact, not a mother at all. Yet on a common-sense understanding of motherhood, of course the woman whose fertilised egg develops into a child is in some important sense that child's mother. She may not ever be the child's social mother, but it makes very little sense to say that she is as unrelated to that child as a total stranger.

It might be argued that the problem here is essentially linguistic. Perhaps legal language simply has insufficient elasticity to accommodate the cultural and technological disintegration of the biological nuclear family. The principle of parental exclusivity means that the law has no concept of 'partial' or 'incomplete' motherhood or fatherhood: you either are or are not a child's legal parent. Not only does this inaccurately describe many children's parentage; it is also out of step with prevalent non-legal understandings of parenthood. It is certainly not now uncommon for children conceived sexually to have more than one man who might be identified as their father, and/or more than one mother-figure. Millions of children have a stepfather *and* a biological father. For children, the presence of multiple parents is undoubtedly less confusing than the law's denial of their existence.

In essence, the principle of parental exclusivity fails to distinguish between two related but different aspects of parenthood: the status of *being a parent* and the power (or duty) to *act as a parent*. Of course, in the paradigm case, these two features of parenthood are inevitably blurred because the power to act *as* a parent derives precisely from *being* a parent. But where the normal incidents of parenthood are distributed between a number of different individuals, while not all of them will have the power to act *as* a parent, each one *is*, in some sense at least, a parent.

In fact, although the principle of parental exclusivity is indeed deeply entrenched, the law already distinguishes between the status of being a parent and the power to act as a parent, through possession of parental responsiblity. To be a parent is to have a connection with your offspring that will endure throughout both your lifetimes. Parental responsibility, on the other hand, is a more transitory and flexible concept. It will last only during the child's minority, and it can be acquired by a variety of non-parents. Anyone who is granted a residence order automatically also gains parental responsibility for the duration of the order,[26] so step-parents or grandparents can be granted parental responsibility despite not being the child's legal parents. Parental responsibility can also vest with a local authority after a child has been taken into care. Mothers (and in some circumstances fathers) will continue to have parental responsibility despite its acquisition by other parties. Thus, the number of people who can have parental responsibility for a child is not limited in the same way as the number of people who can be identified as the child's legal parents.

Parental responsibility is, in essence, the right and duty to look after a child during childhood. It includes, for example, the right to give consent to a child's medical treatment and to take decisions about education. In contrast to parenthood, parental responsibility – with its capacity to be shared, transferred and acquired – is flexible enough to accommodate the social reality of the child's domestic circumstances where these do not conform to the traditional nuclear family. A social 'parent' does not have to become a legal parent in order to offer a child the security and support the child needs. By severing parenthood from parental responsibility, the law has acknowledged that the biological model of family life in which each child lives with her genetic mother and father no longer fits the complex and multiple parent-like relationships that a child may form during life. My proposal in this chapter is that we should take this existing legal recognition of parental variety a stage further.

The law has tended to assume that the bundle of legal rights and duties that *normally* flow from being a parent do so *necessarily*, so that recognising someone's parental status would automatically vest that person with a range of powers and obligations which might – in the case of a sperm donor, for instance – be inappropriate. But the rule that everyone who is recognised as a parent is under an obligation to maintain their child until adulthood is a legal creation rather than a natural consequence of human reproduction. It would be perfectly possible to fix only certain parents with duties of support, or rights to be involved in the child's upbringing.

We already have an example of legislation which facilitates the purely symbolic acknowledgment of a parental bond. Under the Human Fertilisation and Embryology (Deceased Fathers) Act 2003, it is possible for a man to be registered as the father of a child conceived after his death. The recognition of these deceased

---

26 Children Act 1989, s 12.

fathers' paternity is only for the purpose of registration on the child's birth certificate. None of the other normal incidents of paternity, such as inheritance rights, apply, thus avoiding the problem of testamentary uncertainty that might arise if a child could be conceived many years after the father's death. For my purposes, the importance of this Act is its introduction of a new sort of parental status which is limited to the *acknowledgment* of paternity. Obviously none of the rights and duties that normally flow from being a parent can apply to these deceased fathers; instead, the Act simply allows the reality that these children *did* have fathers to be formally recognised. Lifting the numerical restriction upon the number of parents a child might have would enable this sort of symbolic recognition of parenthood to be extended to other 'parents'.

The law has also already taken one small step away from the biological model of legal parenthood through the rules governing the paternity of children born following the artificial insemination, in licensed clinics, of women without husbands or consenting opposite-sex partners. Despite having a biological father, these children are legally *fatherless*: their mother is their only legal parent. Could we further extend this recognition that the 'natural' two-parent family is not always an appropriate way to describe the parentage of a child? Might the law additionally recognise that, in certain circumstances, a child has *more* than one mother or father?

Non-exclusive parenthood?

In sum, acknowledging that the normal features that we associate with being a parent might be distributed among a number of individuals poses two important questions for the law. First, how should we choose which of the various possible 'parents' should also acquire the right and duty to care for and support the child? And second, having singled out the principal parent(s), exactly what is the status of the other individuals who possess one or more parental characteristics? Neither question is at all easy to answer, but my point has been that we should admit that these are matters of choice and judgment, rather than hiding behind a superficially factual inquiry into the identity of a child's parents.

So, for example, making the intention to become a parent the decisive factor in allocating the rights and duties of parenthood following an IVF surrogacy arrangement would be synonymous with making surrogacy contracts specifically enforceable. But if gestation determines the identity of the principal mother, then we are deciding that surrogate mothers should always have the right to change their mind. My purpose here is not to express an opinion on either option, but rather to point out that our current preference for gestation reflects our *decision* to give surrogate mothers the right to renege on their agreements. It may be more convenient to say that the gestational mother is the only mother, and that the woman who contributed the egg and instigated the conception is therefore a stranger to the child, but the price to be paid for this simplicity is a fundamental misrepresentation of a reality of this child's parentage.

The recognition of multiple parents certainly more accurately describes the parenthood of children born following gamete donation. A sperm donor is, in an important sense, the child's genetic father, but this does not necessarily mean that he should have parental responsibility, or owe any other obligations to 'his' child. Instead, by signing the requisite consent form, he has voluntarily agreed to give up *any* parental rights and obligations, and the couple or individual who received treatment have (also by signing the requisite consent form) voluntarily agreed to assume full responsibility for the child from birth. It is therefore only the intended parents who possess the rights and duties we associate with parenthood. Acknowledging the paternity of the sperm donor is especially important given the removal of donor anonymity in April 2005.[27] In the future, children may trace and meet their gamete donors, making acknowledgment of their parenthood, albeit only in a genetic sense, more important. But if the law were capable of recognising multiple parents, this need not displace the parental rights and obligations of the intended or social parents.

Following surrogacy, acknowledging the existence of multiple parents might also be advantageous. When a child is born as the result of a surrogacy agreement, the couple or individual who recruited the surrogate mother are the intended, and often also the genetic, parents, and either of these tests could be sufficient to allow them to be recognised as the child's parents from birth. Of course, the surrogate mother will always be the child's gestational mother, and will sometimes additionally be genetically related to the child. She undoubtedly also has a compelling claim to have her maternity formally acknowledged. In most surrogacy arrangements, where the surrogate is happy to hand over the child at birth, a non-exclusive model of parenthood would permit the commissioning mother and father to be recognised as the child's parents with parental responsibility from birth. The surrogate mother would continue to be the child's birth mother, but she would have voluntarily waived all of the rights and duties we would normally associate with parenthood. Parental duties would instead vest only in the couple or individual with whom the child will be living.

But if the surrogate mother changes her mind about handing over the child, my model would lead us to ask which of the child's parents should possess the rights and obligations of parenthood. The answer to this question depends upon whether one believes that surrogacy contracts should be specifically enforceable or not. If the arguments in favour of specific enforcement are preferred, we could say that the commissioning couple should *always* be recognised as the child's parents with parental responsibility. It might, for example, be argued that the surrogate mother agreed to waive her acquisition of parental responsibility and the other incidents of parental status, in the same way as a sperm or egg donor, and that her agreement should likewise be binding upon her. The commissioning couple's agreement to assume responsibility for the child's upbringing might also be enforceable, so that a man like John Buzzanca would not be permitted to shrug off his obligations towards a child whose conception he instigated. But if specific enforcement is believed to be intrusive, oppressive or otherwise undesirable, parental responsibility could vest initially in the woman from whose body the

27 Human Fertilisation and Embryology Authority (Disclosure of Donor Information) Regulations 2004, SI 2004/1511.

child emerges. She would then continue to have the right to renege on her agreement to relinquish her parental responsibility.

If a surrogate mother changes her mind about handing over the child to the commissioning parents, we cannot avoid the need to *choose* where the child should live. No test for the identification of parents is capable of effacing the human tragedy of this sort of dispute. There is no easy or obviously right solution; rather, when surrogacy agreements break down, the party who is deprived of 'their' child will inevitably suffer profound distress. Whether we decide that the 'losing' party should be the surrogate mother or the commissioning couple, their disappointment will be intense. I would, however, maintain that the 'losing' party should be entitled to recognition, albeit largely symbolic, of their parental status. If the child is to be brought up by the surrogate mother, it might nevertheless be important for that child to know something of the circumstances of her conception, especially since at least one of the intended parents will normally also be genetically related to her. When the child reaches adulthood, the intended parents' identity might be revealed. If the commissioning couple's claim is preferred, the gestational mother's identity might again be disclosed when the child reaches the age of majority. It is worth restating, however, that very few surrogate mothers change their minds. So, while I admit that my proposed shift towards the recognition of multiple parents is incapable of providing a solution to disputed surrogacy arrangements, it would solve the much more common practical problem that arises following surrogate births, namely the need for the child's parentage to be transferred formally via judicial proceedings. Because, as we saw earlier, this cumbersome legal process creates an incentive for informal transfers, unknown numbers of children are currently living with 'parents' who may not have any legal obligations towards them.

It is important to remember that the recognition of multiple parents would not only apply when the normal features of parenthood are split by collaborative reproduction. A non-exclusive model of parenthood might also add clarity to cases of disputed paternity, because it would allow us to admit that a child may have *two* fathers, one genetic and one social. Once doubt has been cast upon the genetic paternity of a child's 'father', I would agree that it is invariably in the child's best interests to have the genetic parentage revealed by blood tests. The advantage of non-exclusive parenthood would be that acknowledging the genetic paternity of the mother's ex-lover need not displace the paternity of the social father. On the contrary, as a result of his ongoing relationship with 'his' child, the social father should be formally recognised as the only legal father who *also* has parental responsibility. In *Re H (Blood Tests: Parental Rights)*,[28] Ward LJ struggled to achieve precisely this sort of result. He argued that 'the issue of biological parentage should be divorced from psychological parentage'. A direction for blood tests was issued because the child's knowing the truth about his genetic paternity would not necessarily 'undermine his attachment to his father figure and he will cope with knowing that *he has two fathers*'[29] (my emphasis). But because,

---

28 [1996] 3 WLR 505, p 523.
29 *Ibid.*

under English law, the discovery that the mother's ex-lover is her son's genetic father completely displaces the social father's 'paternity', the only way in which he could retain parental responsibility would be to apply for a residence order for 'his' child. A better solution, and one that Ward LJ himself appears to endorse, would be to admit evidence that the ex-lover is the genetic father, but to simultaneously affirm the social father's status as the only *father* who also possesses the rights and obligations of parenthood.

Of course, recognising multiple parents will leave us with some extremely difficult questions. We would, for example, have to devise some mechanism for choosing which of the various individuals who possess the normal incidents of parenthood should be principally responsible for the child's upbringing. My point is that we are already making these difficult decisions, but we are hiding them behind the supposedly neutral, objective and purely factual inquiry into the identity of a child's parents.

Conclusion: A right to know the identity of all of your parents?

A child's 'right to know and be cared for by his or her parents' is enshrined in Article 7(1) of the United Nations Convention on the Rights of the Child. While the Convention was ratified by the UK in 1991, it has not been directly incorporated into English law. Nevertheless, the concept of a right to know the identity of one's parents has received judicial approval[30] and may additionally be protected by the right to respect for private and family life, now guaranteed by article 8 of the Human Rights Act 1998. In the words of Wall J, '[k]nowledge of their paternity is increasingly seen not only as a matter of prime importance to children, but as being both their *right* and in their interests'[31] (my emphasis). Obviously, giving effect to this right is only possible if we have a clear understanding of what defines a parent. The UN Convention on the Rights of the Child does not offer any definition, which either could mean that its drafters assumed that a child's parentage would be a self-evident question of fact, or could indicate that states have a 'margin of appreciation' in the rules governing the identification of parents. Importantly, the right to know the identity of one's parents does not necessarily imply any numerical limit upon the number of parents that might exist. Moreover, no practical rights or obligations automatically flow from the right simply to know the identity of one's parents.

Of course, one consequence of a non-exclusive model of parenthood would be that a child's birth certificate might have to record more than one mother and/or father. However counter-intuitive this might initially seem, my point is simply that some children *do* have more than one mother or father, and that by failing to acknowledge this, and to address its practical consequences, the law is unable to adapt to the complexity of family life in the twenty-first century. While the idea

---

30 See, for example, *S v McC (orse S) and M (D S intervener); W v W* [1972] AC 24; *In re G (A Minor) (Parental Responsibility)* [1994] 2 FCR 1037; *In re H (A Minor) (Blood Tests: Parental Rights)* [1996] 3 WLR 506.

31 *In re O (A Minor) (Blood Tests: Constraint)* [2000] Fam 139, p 144.

of parenthood as a divisible status would, in some respects, be a radical departure for the law, given that parenthood now *is* a divisible status, rethinking the legal conception of parenthood is a necessary, albeit difficult, task. Transparency and descriptive accuracy demand that the law relinquishes its principle of parental exclusivity in favour of a model of parenthood that is capable of accommodating its social and technical fragmentation. If people no longer reproduce and raise children within the conventional biological nuclear family, the law should stop pretending that the answer to the question 'What is a parent?' is a fact waiting to be discovered. Rather, however challenging, the law should address the messy reality of multiple parent–child bonds and relationships.

References

Bainham, A (1999) 'Parentage, parenthood and parental responsibility: Subtle, elusive yet important distinctions', in Bainham, A, Sclater, S and Richards, M (eds) *What is a Parent: A Socio-Legal Analysis*, Oxford: Hart Publishing

Bartlett, K (1984) 'Rethinking parenthood as an exclusive status: The need for legal alternatives when the premise of the nuclear family has failed', 70 *Virginia Law Review* 879

Brazier, M, Campbell, A and Golombok, S (1998) *Surrogacy: Review for Health Ministers of Current Arrangements for Payments and Regulation*, London: HMSO (Cm 4068)

Hill, J Lawrence (1991) 'What does it mean to be a 'Parent'? The claims of biology as the basis for parental rights', 66 *New York University Law Review* 353

Human Fertilisation and Embryology Authority (HFEA) (2004) *Code of Practice*, 6th edn, London: HFEA

Shultz, M (1990) 'Reproductive technology and intent-based parenthood: An opportunity for gender neutrality', [1990] *Wisconsin Law Review* 297

Parents in Law: Subjective Impacts and Status Implications around the Use of Licensed Donor Insemination
Caroline Jones

The difference with donor insemination is you will never be the same again . . . *You will never ever be back in the mainstream in totality*, and it changes everything forever. Whereas IVF is a *temporary deviation* down the route to creating *your own family* and carrying off into the sunset.[1]

Introduction

Claire's comment reflects the assumption that most families have a genetic link between parents and their children and indicates her concurrent anxiety about the use of this procedure with her partner Neil. Claire suggests that there is a distinction between heterosexual couples[2] who utilise IVF (crucially when the sperm and ova of the intending parents are used) to create their *own* family, and others who use donor insemination to create families who do not conform to this norm. In construing IVF as a *temporary deviation* in creating a family of one's own, Claire's comment is an acknowledgment of the pervasiveness of 'the family' norm in late twentieth-century British society, where bio-genetic[3] relatedness provides the basis for familial relations. Bio-genetic relatedness may be *actual* – that is, genetic – or *assumed*, on the basis of the relationship between the parents,[4] whether socially or for the purpose of establishing legal parenthood. However, Claire suggests that, when using donor insemination, heterosexual couples cannot simply 'carry off into the sunset'. Rather, this procedure disrupts the bio-genetic link between social fathers and their children. Hence, bio-genetic ties are no longer taken for granted, but must be managed or negotiated.

The 'need' for the management of donor-conceived family ties has been noted in academic commentaries on kinship and the legal regulation of assisted reproduction. For example, Erica Haimes[5] argues that the 'transgression of assumed familial forms' (ie, the absence of a bio-genetic link between parent(s) and children

---

1 Claire, interviewee (emphasis added).
2 When asked during the interview, Claire confirmed that she was specifically referring to couples in heterosexual relationships. For the purpose of brevity I use the phrase 'heterosexual couples' here.
3 As Day Sclater, Bainham and Richards (1999), p 15 argue, social parenting aside, Anglo-Welsh law has increasingly drawn on the concept of biological parenthood with regard to the familial relations between parents and children. However, given the distinction between genetic and gestational motherhood for example, 'biological' parenthood requires clarification in legal discourse (Johnson (1999), pp 49–58). Hence my preferred term is 'bio-genetic' parenthood.
4 Smart (1987), p 114; Bainham (1999), p 26.
5 Haimes (2002), p 444.

in families conceived through donation) requires social management. While Haimes's[6] focus is on the anonymity of gamete donors rather than naming practices *per se*, she is clear that: 'The nature of that [social] management is highly significant since it reflects and affects the way a society thinks about individuals, parents, children and families.' In the context of Haimes's discussion, donor anonymity is perceived as a regulatory mechanism which can simultaneously facilitate families with children conceived by donation to pass as 'the family' whilst arguably protecting the best interests of the child and the donor.[7] Hence, the practice of donor anonymity both mirrors and reinforces the 'problematic' status of transgressive donor-conceived families.[8] The focus of this chapter, however, is the significance of the legal ascription of parenthood, in the context of donor insemination, as a mechanism of the social management of family formation. Identifying a particular person as a legal parent, or excluding another from parental status, can clearly both affect and reflect societal attitudes to parenting and transgressive familial forms; hence Haimes's comments remain salient in this context.[9]

The focus of my discussion is the impact of the legal ascription of parenthood upon establishing familial status and associated kinship naming practices in both lesbian and heterosexual families with children conceived by donation.[9a] I begin by considering the authority of legal discourse to confer parenthood when licensed donor insemination[10] is used. Hence, I examine some of the ways in which Anglo-Welsh discourse 'matches', for the purposes of legal parenthood, social fathers to donor-conceived children and yet denies similar status to co-mothers. It is important to note the terminology used here. The kinship terms used to refer to a mother's lesbian partner who also shares a parenting role in a particular child's life have been discussed by a number of feminist commentators.[11] Where donor insemination is used, the terminology is particularly significant, as the co-mother is not replacing another parent (ie biological or social father). I have elected to use 'co-mother' rather than 'co-parent' to highlight the issue of gender, concurrently rendering visible the role of these women and highlighting the way in which Anglo-Welsh legal discourse has tended to marginalise them through a process of exclusion.

I then consider the interview accounts of four lesbian couples and two heterosexual couples who had undertaken donor insemination at licensed British clinics in the 1990s. An analysis of their accounts facilitates an understanding of the *subjective* impact of the legal ascription of parenthood (or lack thereof) for some

---

6 *Ibid.*

7 Haimes (2002), pp 444–6; also Haimes (1990), pp 167–8.

8 However, from 1 April 2005 donor anonymity was removed (the Human Fertilisation and Embryology Authority (Disclosure of Donor Information) Regulations 2004, SI 2004/1511).

9 See also Jackson, Chapter 4 in this volume.

9a Elsewhere I have considered the construction of implied bio-genetic links between donor-conceived children and co-mothers, and to co-mothers' extended families, see Jones (2005).

10 This refers to donor insemination undertaken at a fertility clinic licensed by the Human Fertilisation and Embryology Authority and therefore regulated by the Human Fertilisation and Embryology Act 1990.

11 Hayden (1995); Gabb (1999); Comeau (1999).

persons using donor insemination to create their families. An examination of my interviewees' comments regarding the legal status of the (male or female) co-parent and the kinship terminology they use within their families demonstrates the normative effects of, *and* strategic resistance to, the (lack of) legal recognition for a particular parent. A clear distinction is drawn between one form of legal recognition – the statutory requirements regarding the registration of a child's birth – and its subjective effects, including the democratic processes of kinship naming practices undertaken within lesbian families by donation in different contexts (including within their families, at a licensed clinic and at a doctor's surgery). The latter practices, it is argued, are particularly revealing with regard to 'status' concerns for families that transgress assumed familial forms. These status implications raised in my interviewees' accounts pose three interrelated questions: the first is whether Anglo-Welsh family law has the necessary mechanisms for recognising the parental role of co-mothers; the second is whether the legal concept of 'parenthood' is even an appropriate status to reflect the role of co-mothers; and the third is the way in which lesbian (co-)motherhood might be accommodated under the current law relating to parenthood.

Ascribing legal parenthood

Anglo-Welsh law requires parents to register their child's birth within 42 days.[12] Where the child's parents are unmarried, the onus lies solely on the mother.[13] However, as Bainham[14] has noted, there is no requirement that the mother register the father's name. The current statutory provisions relating to the circumstances which permit unmarried fathers' registration are contained in s 10(1)(a)–(d), s 10(1A) and s 10A(1A) Births and Deaths Registration Act 1953, as amended. A child's birth certificate is a shortened version of the details provided in the birth register, including the place and date of birth, and the names of the child's registered parent(s). Consequently the registration of the child's birth provides a 'historical' (legal) claim of parental status (or 'parentage').[15] In the context of assisted reproduction where donor gametes are used, this 'historical' status simultaneously excludes others, who may be bio-genetically related to the child, from making this claim. This is particularly significant, as being named on the child's birth certificate provides an almost inalienable link between parent and donor-conceived child. Parental status can be terminated only by a successful application for an adoption order,[16] or a parental order.[17]

However, parental status is also crucially important because of the legal effects attached to being a parent, which non-parents, who may nevertheless perform a

---

12 Births and Deaths Registration Act 1953, s 2.
13 Births and Deaths Registration Act 1953, s 10(1).
14 Bainham (1999), p 43.
15 See Bridge (1999).
16 The provisions contained in the Adoption Act 1976 have been superseded by the Adoption and Children Act 2002.
17 Where surrogacy is involved, see Human Fertilisation and Embryology Act 1990, s 30.

parental role in a particular child's life, can neither exercise nor claim *as of right*.[18] I focus on two of these effects, namely the allocation of parental responsibility and the membership in a family.[19]

Parental responsibility is automatically accorded to married fathers[20] irrespective of whether or not they have a bio-genetic tie to the child.[21] Adoption and Children Act 2002 s 111, amending s 4 Children Act 1989, provides that, upon joint registration with the mother, unmarried fathers also have parental responsibility for their children.[22] Hence, the ascription of parental status arguably provides the simplest way of allocating parental responsibility (although it remains possible for unmarried fathers to seek a 'parental responsibility agreement' with the child's mother,[23] to apply to the court for a parental responsibility order,[24] or to be awarded parental responsibility attached to a residence order).[25] While it is possible for non-parents, including lesbian co-mothers, to be allocated parental responsibility by being granted a joint residence order,[26] this is limited to the duration of the residence order and will, in any event, terminate when the child reaches majority.[27] In contrast, *being* a parent is a lifelong status and concurrently determines which family a child is legally considered to be a member of, an issue which, as Andrew Bainham[28] points out, has often been overlooked. However, in the Court of Appeal decision in *Re R (a child)*, Hale LJ (as she then was) drew attention to this very issue, stating:

> [S]ection 28(3) [HFEA 1990] is an unusual provision, conferring the relationship of parent and child on people who are related neither by blood nor by marriage. Conferring such relationships is a serious matter, involving as it does not only the relationship between father and child *but also between the whole of the father's family*

---

18 Bainham (1999), pp 33–4, lists these effects.

19 With regard to the ambit of parental responsibility, see Herring (2004), pp 256–66.

20 Children Act 1989, s 2(1).

21 Human Fertilisation and Embryology Act 1990, s 28(2).

22 Children Act 1989, s 4(1)(a): see Sheldon (2001); Wallbank (2002). However, Children Act 1989 s 2A provides that parental responsibility acquired under s 4 can be removed by a court order.

23 Children Act 1989, s 4(1)(b).

24 Children Act 1989, s 4(1)(c).

25 Children Act 1989, s 12(1).

26 Children Act 1989, s 12(2): see *Re C (A Minor) (Residence Order: Lesbian Co-parents)* [1994] Fam Law 468 (unreported elsewhere); *G v F (Contact and Shared Residence: Applications for leave)* [1998] 2 FLR 799; and now *Re G (Children)* [2005] EWCA Civ 462. Co-mothers (and other non-parents) who cannot satisfy the terms of Children Act 1989 s 10(5)(b), which requires the child to have lived with that person for a period of at least three years, have to apply to the court for leave in order to make the application under s 8 Children Act 1989. From 30 December 2005 it has been possible for step-parents to seek parental responsibility under s 4A(1) Children Act 1989, as amended. However, this is limited to those persons who have married or undertaken a civil partnership with the child's parent(s).

27 Hence, the provisions permitting same-sex adoption (ie by both partners) under the Adoption and Children Act 2002 are to be welcomed, as this ensures parental responsibility *and* parental status.

28 Bainham (1999), p 33.

and the child. The rule should only apply to those cases which clearly fall within the footprint of the statutory language (para 20).[29]

This judgment clearly acknowledges that the 'historical' claim to parental status goes far beyond determining the legal recognition of a particular parent–child relationship; it also determines one's kinship status in and to that parent's wider family. For the registration of the birth of a donor-conceived child, where different persons may make competing claims of 'parenthood', it is particularly significant to determine who is considered to be the legal mother or father.

Statutory provisions: the Family Law Reform Act 1987[30]

Traditionally, fathers were 'matched' with children through their marital relationship with the mother, being named as the father upon registration of the child's birth, and the concurrent assumption of a bio-genetic tie to the child. Some feminist legal commentators suggested that donor insemination was considered problematic, as the notion of the 'child of the marriage' was potentially undermined by the lack of a bio-genetic tie between husband and donor-conceived child.[31] However, Snowden and Mitchell[32] suggested that where donor insemination was used, married social fathers' names were 'almost invariably' entered as the father on the child's birth certificate. This practice was sanctioned by s 27 Family Law Reform Act 1987, which provided that, when donor insemination was used, married social fathers were to be considered the legal father of the donor-conceived child. Hence, s 27(1) Family Law Reform Act 1987 *explicitly extended* the notion of the 'child of the marriage' to incorporate donor-conceived children. It is possible to view this extension as a reiteration of 'the family' norm, in light of its potential erosion through involuntary childlessness or the (previously) illegitimate status of children conceived through the use of donor sperm. The extension of this legal concept also established connections between married men and their donor-conceived children for the purposes of property and inheritance[33] and ensured that men, as fathers, retained financial (and arguably emotional) responsibilities for children.[34] However, developments in assisted reproductive technologies, which prompted wider issues than matching children to fathers, led to the introduction of comprehensive legislation to regulate these procedures and the legal ascription of parenthood for resultant children.

---

29 [2003] EWCA Civ 182, [2003] Fam 129, [2003] 2 All ER 131 (emphasis added). See Sheldon (2005); Lind (2003). The High Court decision in this case was reported as *Re D (Parental Responsibility: IVF baby)* [2001] 1 FLR 972. In May 2005, the Court of Appeal decision was upheld in the House of Lords, and reported as *Re D (a child appearing by her guardian ad litem)* [2005] UKHL 33.

30 See also Jackson, Chapter 4 in this volume.

31 Pfeffer (1987), p 94; for an anthropological account, see Strathern (1992).

32 Snowden and Mitchell (1981), p 17.

33 Smart (1987), pp 99–101.

34 Wallbank (2001).

Statutory provisions: the Human Fertilisation and Embryology Act 1990

Sarah Franklin[35] provides a feminist anthropological analysis of the parliamentary debates on the Human Fertilisation and Embryology Bill,[36] highlighting the authority of legal discourse in this respect. Franklin[37] discusses the social construction of 'natural' facts in the context of kinship and legal parenthood. She argues:

> The order of nature provides the basis or foundation for the order of law in the definition of kinship ties. True to the consistent attribution of privileged authority to clinical and scientific expertise throughout the debates, 'natural facts' . . . were seen to provide the neutral, impartial and objective facts of the matter upon which legislation should properly be based.[38]

However, Franklin cautions that the invocation of 'natural' facts in the HFE Bill parliamentary debates is limited. At times, 'natural' facts are 'displaced',[39] and at other junctures, 'lost'.[40] Franklin's argument is exemplified by reference to the meaning ascribed to 'mother' in what would become s 27 Human Fertilisation Embryology Act 1990.[41] She notes: 'Here, the dilemma of assisted nature resides in the emergence of two "natural" mothers: the genetic and the birth mother. Who is the "real" mother? Nature cannot referee.'[42] With this legislation, the birth mother is designated the legal mother, and the significance of genetic links between mothers and children is marginalised. Hence, legal discourse is able to make claims of 'truth' with regard to the ascription of parenthood. Consequently, alternative constructions of 'mother' are disqualified for the purposes of legal status and rights in relation to the donor-conceived child.[43]

With respect to the legal designation of the 'father' of donor-conceived children, Franklin states that:

> [T]he authority of nature was simply abandoned . . . gamete donors' . . . 'natural' parenthood was rendered legally unrecognisable. Likewise in granting to husbands of women recipients of donor insemination the right to register their name as father on the birth certificate, *the law takes on new powers of conferring parental status*.[44]

HFEA 1990 s 28(2) authorises women's husbands – who may or may not intend to become social fathers – to be entered as the 'father' on the child's birth certificate.[45]

---

35 Franklin (1993).
36 Hereafter HFE Bill.
37 Franklin (1993), pp 103–5.
38 *Ibid*, p 104.
39 Franklin (1993, p 104) cites embryo research and the limitation of 14 days imposed in the HFE Bill (s 3) as an example. That is, the *actual* emergence of the primitive streak in a particular embryo is displaced in favour of a blanket limitation period for all embryos.
40 Franklin (1993), p 104.
41 Hereafter HFEA 1990.
42 Franklin (1993), p 104.
43 See also Jackson, Chapter 4 in this volume.
44 Franklin (1993), p 105 (emphasis added).
45 The presumption of paternity is rebuttable if the husband can show he did not consent to the insemination (see also Schedule 3 HFEA 1990; Lee and Morgan (2001), p 237).

Similarly, s 28(3) HFEA 1990 provides for unmarried male partners treated 'together' with the legal mother to be named 'father' on a donor-conceived child's birth certificate.[46] Hence, it is clear that Anglo-Welsh legal discourse may privilege a particular construction of the 'father' of a donor-conceived child. In so doing, genetic links between sperm donors and children are also disqualified as significant markers of parenthood. However, in light of the recent change in policy regarding donor anonymity it would seem that attitudes have subsequently shifted in this area.[47] Nevertheless, no legal status or obligations will be provided for sperm (or egg or embryo) donors as a consequence of the removal of anonymity. Consequently, for the purposes of the *legal* ascription of parenthood of donor-conceived children, bio-genetic ties remain marginalised under the current legal provisions.

Franklin concludes:

> To argue simply that the law in such cases explicitly supersedes (or 'assists') in the social construction of natural facts to an unprecedented degree is not enough, since, by definition, a law designed to establish regulatory control over 'human fertilisation and embryology' could do little else.[48]

It is conceded that the HFEA 1990 probably could do little else. However, it does not follow that the provisions of ss 27 and 28 HFEA 1990 were the only solution(s) to the complications of social and legal parenthood prompted by assisted reproductive technologies, nor that Anglo-Welsh law had necessarily to deal with the issues raised by these procedures in the ways that it did. As a consequence of s 28 HFEA 1990, social fathers (and their families) are clearly matched to their donor-conceived children, named as such on the child's birth certificate, and can exercise parental responsibility (subject to s 4 Children Act 1989). In contrast, lesbian co-mothers are marginalised through a process of exclusion whereby they have no route to parental status. They cannot be named on the child's birth certificate, their donor-conceived children are not legally matched to their wider families, *nor* are they automatically accorded parental responsibility. Therefore, it is clear that it is heterosexual parenthood which is privileged in Anglo-Welsh legal discourse. However, analysis of the legislation alone does not provide space for understanding its subjective impact upon persons undertaking donor insemination.[49] In the next section, I seek to address this lacuna through the examination of the subjective significance of these legal provisions for some users of donor insemination, as reported in their interview accounts. The legal ascription of parenthood was an issue raised by all of my interviewees, some of whom stated that they had sought information about the legal status of each parent when donor insemination was used.

---

46 See *Re D (a child appearing by her guardian ad litem)* [2005] UKHL 33, [2005] FCR 223.
47 See also Wallbank (2004).
48 Franklin (1993), p 105.
49 Probert (2004), p 288.

Subjective impacts

Method

During the period between March and November 1999, I undertook a total of nine semi-structured interviews with women and men who had sought access to licensed donor insemination following the enactment of the 1990 Act. The sample comprised three lesbian couples and one woman in a lesbian relationship whose partner did not attend the interview; two married heterosexual couples; and three single women (whom I will not be discussing in this chapter). Consequently, this small sample is intended to be illustrative rather than representative of the 'population' of users of licensed donor insemination in Britain. I established contact with this sample through the use of gatekeepers, notably Lisa Saffron, who has published widely on self-insemination in particular,[50] and the (then) Donor Insemination Network,[51] which has been re-named the Donor Conception Network.[52] All interviewees were aged between their late 20s and mid-40s, and most presented themselves as being middle class in terms of their current standard of living. All the women interviewed were white, although one woman indicated that her female partner (who was not present) was African Caribbean. In order to maintain the anonymity of the accounts provided, all interviewees have been assigned pseudonyms.

Interviewees' responses to the legal ascription of fatherhood

Claire and Neil initially sought access to donor insemination in the late 1980s, prior to the HFEA 1990. Under the Anglo-Welsh legal provisions at that time,[53] Neil would have been recognised as the legal father of any child resulting from donor insemination. Consequently, Neil could legally be named as the father on the child's birth certificate.[54] This naming was clearly crucial for Claire and Neil, as the following exchange indicates:

Claire: We had looked at the law and we knew that children, we knew that in April 1987 they became, you [Neil] became the legal father on the birth certificate. Prior to that you had to lie. So we knew that, which was helpful. From our point of view that was quite significant because . . .

Neil: Well we didn't want to lie because we were being open [about using donor insemination].

Claire: Otherwise it was illegitimate. I think it was illegitimate wasn't it? *You either lied or they wrote illegitimate on it and we didn't want an illegitimate child.*[55]

---

50 Saffron (1994; 1996; 1998; 2001).
51 www.issue.co.uk/dinet (last accessed 2001).
52 www.dcnetwork.org/ (last accessed September 2005).
53 Family Law Reform Act, s 27(1).
54 This aspect of the Family Law Reform Act 1987 was incorporated into HFEA 1990, s 28(2).
55 Emphasis added.

Claire and Neil highlight the legal changes made by the Family Law Reform Act 1987, which sought to remove the use of labels like 'illegitimate'.[56] As outlined above, naming Neil the legal father put him in the same position legally (in terms of his status to the child), as he would have been had the child had been conceived from his own sperm. Crucially, Neil could attain this status on the basis of his marriage to Claire.

Claire and Neil indicated that, following the birth of their first child, they were open about the use of donor sperm and had informed their son and their families of his means of conception. In addition, Claire and Neil had participated in numerous press interviews. This would suggest that they had little concern for maintaining secrecy around their use of donor insemination. Claire and Neil did not appear anxious to 'pass' as 'the family', in contrast to a family-by-donation. Rather, it would seem that they were more concerned with the possibility of openness around their use of donor sperm. In addition, given Claire's emphasis on illegitimacy, the legal status of the child and the potential stigma of illegitimacy were clearly important considerations.

A number of feminist legal commentators have noted the 'quasi-illegitimate' status of donor children prior to the Family Law Reform Act 1987 and HFEA 1990.[57] Snowden and Mitchell, on the other hand, have argued that often it is the '*charge*' of illegitimacy in relation to the child [that] is more important than the fact of illegitimacy'.[58] The notion of the 'charge' of illegitimacy is significant. This indicates that discourse operates through an 'economy' of truth, whereby one form of 'truth' is privileged over alternatives. Hence, prior to the Family Law Reform Act 1987, legal discourse named the married heterosexual family as '*legitimate*', thereby normalising this particular family form and marginalising 'other' families. Claire and Neil's account indicates that the normalisation of the legitimate family in legal discourse is crucial. The 'fact' of illegitimacy is not a problem for them, it is accepted; Claire and Neil indicated they made no attempt to conceal their use of donor insemination (either within or outwith their family), but they expressed concern over the 'label' or *charge* of illegitimacy in legal, and concurrently social, discourse. This suggests that Claire and Neil attached particular importance to the authority of Anglo-Welsh legal discourse in their subjective experience of a 'legitimate' parental status.

Lisa and David also emphasised the significance of legally naming David as the donor-conceived child's 'father' on the birth certificate. David noted:

> I think I wouldn't have been very happy at all going along and registering the birth as the father *illegally* which I would have been doing until whenever it was when the Act changed that. Because there was one lady [at the Donor Conception Network] who talked about how she *broke the law* [pre-Family Law Reform Act 1987]. So I knew that legally, in the eyes of the law, [post-HFEA 1990] that was all clear cut.[59]

---

56 Hoggett (1993), p 28.
57 Blythe and Moore (2001), p 221; Jackson (2001), p 165.
58 Snowden and Mitchell (1981), pp 35–6, original emphasis.
59 Emphasis added.

David expresses relief that he could legally register himself as the child's father. In fact, David's actions in registering himself as the 'father' on the child's birth certificate are equivalent to those of the woman he mentions at the Donor Conception Network. In both cases, the social father was registered as 'the' father on a donor-conceived child's birth certificate, thereby occluding the identity of the bio-genetic father. However, as David's child was conceived and born following the enactment of the HFEA 1990, his actions were explicitly legally sanctioned. This clearly highlights the authority of Anglo-Welsh legal discourse to ascribe, or deny, parental status to particular legal subjects and also points to the historical specificity of discursive constructions.[60]

At the time the Family Law Reform Act 1987 and HFEA 1990 were passed through Parliament, there was considerable political interest in child maintenance[61] and the preservation of 'the family' in the context of an increasing number of single-parent families and the development of assisted reproductive technologies.[62] The established legal principles (illegitimacy/legitimacy, and the presumption of paternity in marriage) governing parental status were considered inadequate to deal with the changing demography of families. The legislative changes ensured that children could be 'attached' to fathers regardless of whether they were linked through a bio-genetic tie.[63] It is significant to note that neither Claire and Neil nor Lisa and David mentioned naming practices within their families at any point during the interview. They were pleased that law's ascription of fatherhood confirmed their subjective ascription of fatherhood. This effect lies in clear contrast to the accounts provided by lesbian couples.

Interviewees' responses to the legal ascription of motherhood

> That's another one of the issues that came up at the clinic . . . the secrecy [about the use of donor sperm]. There's an *element of secrecy about it in that normally it's heterosexual couples*, and the husband will be the *legal father*. And of course *we* [Sarah and her partner Kate] *can't pretend* that either one of us is the child's father. There'll be no pretence on that.[64]

Sarah's comment clearly highlights two issues: namely, the legal recognition of a husband's parental status in relation to his donor-conceived child(ren) and the perceived atmosphere of secrecy around the use of donor insemination by heterosexual couples.[65] I read Sarah's comment as an acknowledgment of the discursive construction of the legal 'father' in Anglo-Welsh legal discourse. Sarah implies that this discursive construction facilitates social fathers 'pretending' they are the bio-genetic fathers of donor-conceived children. She also distinguishes between

---

60 Foucault (1980).
61 Wallbank (2001).
62 Smart (1987); Haimes (1990); Jackson (2001).
63 Smart (1987).
64 Sarah, interviewee; emphasis added.
65 The issue of secrecy falls outside the focus of this chapter: see further Snowden and Mitchell (1981); O'Donovan (1988; 1989; 1998); Daniels and Taylor (1993); Golombok *et al* (1996; 2004); Murray and Golombok (2003).

the situation of heterosexual couples and that of lesbian couples using donor insemination. Lesbian couples (including Sarah and her partner Kate) cannot 'pretend' that both parents are biologically related to the child in the way that a heterosexual couple may. Consequently naming practices for lesbian parents must be negotiated in a different legal and social context from that experienced by heterosexual partners. It is one in which their families are marginalised and rendered 'alternative', but it is also one in which there are no pre-existing 'rules' and therefore in which the 'rules' *might* be designed from scratch. It is this space, one in which both normative hostility and transgressive potential must be negotiated, that is informative with regard to status issues for lesbian co-mothers.

Status

Andrea noted the lack of status she was afforded as the child's co-mother:

> It annoys me that [as a co-mother] *you're seen as a nothing*. Do you know what I mean? You've got no legal rights as a parent if you like, like other people have. I'd really like it if like *other couples* you could actually adopt,[66] although I'm another woman, I want to be *sort of a parent*.[67]

There are three interrelated issues raised by Andrea's comment. First, her status as a co-mother is characterised as being insignificant. Second, Andrea contrasts the lack of legal recognition of her parenting role to the rights she perceives are extended to 'other' (ie heterosexual) couples. Finally, in expressing a desire to have formal legal recognition of her parental role – '*to be sort of a parent*' – Andrea's comments highlight the negotiation of kinship terms when articulating issues relating to co-mothers.

Taking together Andrea's first two points, it is not immediately clear whether Andrea's observation that she is 'a nothing' is meant generally at the everyday level (that is, in terms of her assumption of parental responsibilities, and Louise's and their extended families' recognition of her parental role), or strictly in relation to her lack of legal status. However, she states that 'other' couples (couples which I read as heterosexual) are accorded legal recognition of their parental role in relation to donor-conceived children. Hence, it would appear that she is referring to

---

66 Section 50 Adoption and Children Act 2002 provides for same-sex couples to adopt together. For the purposes of s 50, 'a couple' is defined under s 144(4)(b) as 'two people (whether of different sexes or the same sex) living as partners in an enduring family relationship'. It is possible that permitting same-sex adoption could lead to the development of alternative naming practices. For example, a co-mother like Andrea may be more inclined to label herself a 'parent' as opposed to 'sort of a parent'. It is significant to note that the gender-neutral term 'parent(s)' is used in Schedule 1 of the Adopted Children and Adoption Contact Registers Regulations 2005, which governs the form of entry in the Adopted Children Register. Roger Errington, Head of Adoptions at the General Register Office, explains that 'this was the straightforward summary wording which the lawyers were satisfied would cover all possible combinations of adoptive relationship . . . The above use of "parent(s)" replaces the use of "adopter or adopters" currently in use as prescribed by the Forms of Adoption Entry Regulations 1975' (personal communication, 7 September 2005). It is not clear why 'adopter(s)' would not encompass all adoptive relationships. Nevertheless, the use of these gender-neutral terms suggests normative hostility to the possibility of two 'mothers' (or indeed 'fathers') within legal discourse.

67 Emphasis added.

the absence of any legal status as the child's co-mother. The emphasis she places on the significance of formal legal recognition suggests frustration at not being accorded parental status. In addition, it appears to feed into her naming practices, whereby the terms used tend to minimise her role in the child's life, notwithstanding the responsibilities she undertakes daily.[68] Thus, Andrea indicates that legal discourse has a particularly significant authority in assigning rights and status to parents.

Naming practices: 'Parent'

The terminology Andrea uses is indicative of the negotiation of kinship terms relating to co-mothers. Charis Cussins[69] has examined the strategies used by women using assisted reproductive technologies at a US clinic to determine who would be considered the mother of a child resulting from donor eggs and/or the use of (host or full) surrogacy. She has noted that 'legal and familial constraints bring their own forms of *plasticity* and *relative invariance* which are very powerful in determining kin'.[70] Two features of Andrea's account are particularly salient. First, she draws a distinction between her lack of legal rights and those afforded to parents in heterosexual relationships, whose status as 'mother' and 'father' are formally legally recognised (s 27 and s 28 HFEA 1990 respectively). Clearly, legal parenthood is limited to the recognition of one mother and one father.[71] Second, Andrea does not refer to herself as a mother. Rather, she categorises her role with the gender-neutral term 'parent'. She reiterates this later in the interview: 'Obviously Louise is his mum and he will always call Louise his mum, but I am Andrea, I am a parent. I see myself as a parent not another mum.' Therefore, it seems that the 'relative invariance' of the formal recognition of the gestational mother in legal discourse, as well as the legal exclusivity of motherhood, have a powerful normalising effect with regard to the kinship terms used by Andrea.

However, it is *not* only legal discourse which may have a powerful normalising effect with regard to the negotiation of kinship terms for lesbian co-mothers. Gillian Dunne[72] has noted 'the power of ideas about the singularity and the exclusivity of the identity of "Mum" in a social world structured by heterosexual norms that polarise parenting along lines of gender'. The gendered, heteronormative framing of parenting in social and legal discourses clearly can have powerful normalising effects. Andrea does not claim the status of 'mother' in the interview. On the one hand, this is demonstrative of the constraints of language in describing kinship relations in lesbian families resulting from donation. In fact, during the interviews none of the co-mothers claim the term 'mother', although Beverley refers to her partner and co-mother Fiona as the 'other-mother', and Jane

---

68 See the discussion under 'Joint residence orders' below.
69 Cussins (1998); also Thompson (formerly Cussins) (2001).
70 Cussins (1998), p 55, emphasis added.
71 See discussion in Jackson, Chapter 4 in this volume. However, the New Zealand Law Commission recently raised the possibility of a child having more than two legal parents: see New Zealand Law Commission (2005), paras 6.67–6.73 and 8.15–8.17.
72 Dunne (2000), p 24.

refers to Helen, her partner, as 'mummy Helen' (discussed further below). On the other hand, Andrea's use of the term 'parent' could also suggest the possibility that lesbian couples can re-conceptualise kinship terms in ways that are non-gender-specific.[73] Hence, subjects can resist dominant discursive constructions. Consequently, the refusal to use the gendered term 'mother' in this instance can point to the productive potential of discourse and ongoing negotiation of kinship terms. Hence, the authority of legal and social discourse is not absolute, but rather is continually negotiated and renegotiated at the capillary of power relations by particular subjects in specific circumstances.[74]

Alternative strategies for the recognition of a co-mother's parental status

Consenting to insemination

Naming practices not only are significant within families, but can potentially provide external recognition of a co-mother's parental role. Kate and Sarah discussed the strategy they used to provide the co-mother (Sarah) with a symbolic form of recognition of her intending parental role. They noted that, during the process of accessing donor insemination at a licensed clinic, Sarah signed the consent form usually signed by the male partner of a woman undertaking assisted reproductive technologies:

Sarah: Often they [clinic officials] don't know how to treat the co-parent, like on the form you sign they use the term husband for the partner.

Kate: For us they [clinic officials] crossed out 'father' and put 'parent'. We were both signing to say that Sarah also agreed to the treatment and also *recognising Sarah as a parent. It was symbolic*. It's important for the child to know that it was a joint decision.[75]

Signing the consent form is a transgressive practice, which means that subjects like Kate and Sarah are not passive in the process of ascribing parenthood. Rather, they are actively writing themselves into this process at the clinic. As outlined above, s 28(2) and (3) HFEA 1990 provides that when licensed donor insemination is used by heterosexual couples, the husband or male partner will be considered the child's legal father unless he proves he did not consent to the treatment. Hence, husbands or male partners of women undertaking donor insemination are requested to sign an appropriate consent form.[76] This is not 'to make the treatment

---

73 See Dunne (2000) for a discussion of parenting practices that are not necessarily mediated along gender-specific lines, a detailed discussion of which falls outside the focus of this chapter.

74 See Weeks, Heaphy and Donovan (2001) for a discussion of same-sex partners (in Britain) remaking 'family' or 'families of choice', outside of heterosexual norms and legal discourse rooted in those norms. Weeks *et al* note that, while these processes can be difficult for non-heterosexuals, the emergent 'practices of freedom' can also be liberating, and provide ongoing challenges to traditional heterosexual assumptions.

75 Emphasis added.

76 Human Fertilisation and Embryology Authority (2004), paras 7.28–29.

lawful'; rather it is to avoid any 'evidential difficulty' arising in relation to the ascription of the legal father for a resulting child.[77]

Given the significance of the consent form for the legal determination of *father-hood*, it is clear that Kate's and Sarah's practice of jointly signing this form is transgressive, challenging 'the family' norm. Kate's comments suggest that they were aware that by signing this form, Sarah would *not* be ascribed legal parental status in relation to their donor-conceived child. However, it was clearly significant that Sarah be afforded some formal, symbolic recognition of her intention to parent. Hence, Kate's and Sarah's reported practice of signing this form indicates that they were able to mobilise and reconfigure legal consent in ways that ascribed a symbolic recognition of Sarah's co-parenting role, and may be evidence of a form of local and strategic resistance to the dominant norms of consent associated with accessing and using licensed donor insemination. By using the existing legal framework, while at the same time reconfiguring it by having the term 'parent' inserted in the place of 'father', Kate and Sarah challenged the hetero-normative assumption associated with consent for licensed donor insemination. However, there are some limitations to their practice.

The use of the gender-neutral term 'parent' on the consent form is significant. It is not entirely clear who chose this term, as Kate's comments suggest it was the clinic, rather than the couple themselves. If Kate and Sarah chose this term, it could be possible to argue that they can reconfigure the term 'parent' in a positive way. That is, as outlined above, 'parent' could be an example of lesbian couples' reconfiguration of kinship terms in ways that challenge gendered hetero-normative assumptions about mothering and fathering and gender-appropriate parenting roles.[78] However, use of the term 'parent' may also be evidence of law's inability to comprehend a gendered parental status for Sarah, once Kate became a mother. Further, if it was the clinic's choice of kinship term, it is possible to read the gender-neutral term 'parent' as providing a marginal status to subjects like Sarah. That is, those 'parents' who do not conform to 'the family' norm are excluded from claiming the identity 'co-mother' (or even 'mother') on the clinic's consent form. Second, while this practice may provide a challenge to the assumption that only heterosexual couples using licensed donor insemination will sign the consent form for the purposes of eliminating evidential difficulties in relation to the legal ascription of parenthood, because this practice was informal and invisible, insofar as the consent form would not be acknowledged outside the clinic for the purposes of establishing parental status, its transgressive effect is reduced. However, there are two other formal legal provisions which lesbian co-mothers can seek to implement in (partial) recognition of their parental role: joint residence orders and guardianship. Guardianship is significant here insofar as it provides some appreciation of the legal power to designate, even if only after death, a status they have lived and experienced.

---

77 Kennedy and Grubb (1994), p 789; also Jackson (2001), pp 239–40.
78 Dunne (2000).

Joint residence orders

Seeking a joint residence order was an issue raised in all four lesbian couples' accounts. In Jane's and Helen's case, the reason for seeking a joint residence order was explained with reference to co-mother Helen's lack of legal status. At the time of the interview, they had completed an affadavit but not yet begun formal legal proceedings. Earlier in the interview, Jane had noted that, as the birth mother, she had parental responsibility automatically, whereas for Helen she states:

> It [joint residence order] does need to be done, and I think it's more of an issue for you isn't it [to Helen] and also for [daughter] to know that *legally we are both her parents*. That does have a weight and standing actually for a child to know that it's not just mummy Helen who's not really, at the end of the day, *can't sign anything down at the doctor's surgery* to say she can have medication or whatever. *It's important for [daughter] to know that mummy Helen can do all that, as can mummy Jane you know.*[79]

Jane discusses the importance of Helen having parental responsibility in terms of both the symbolic significance and the practical implications this would have for Helen and their daughter. Jane clearly expresses a desire that their daughter would know that she and Helen are *legally* her *parents*, suggesting that legal discourse is a powerful normalising factor in signifying kinship relations within their family,[80] including the emotional and psychological security that might be provided by knowledge of that relationship. But again, in Jane's account, legal recognition is discussed by reference to the gender-neutral term 'parents' rather than in relation to the possible recognition of two 'mothers'. In contrast, when discussing the significance of the legal recognition of Helen's parental role from their *daughter's* perspective, it is interesting to note the shift to the use of the terms 'mummy Jane' and 'mummy Helen'. This subtle shift is significant, as it points concurrently to the singularity of meaning of kinship terms (ie both could not be 'mum') *and* their plasticity, inasmuch as there is the potential for both 'mummy Jane' and 'mummy Helen' to be named as such within one family, even when legal recognition is articulated in the only language in which the law can so far cope with two mothers: as gender-neutral parents.

In terms of the practical significance, parental responsibility confers a range of rights and responsibilities for the child,[81] yet Jane highlights future interactions with the medical profession. On the one hand, this indicates Jane's awareness of the absence of legal rights accorded to Helen. On the other hand, this suggests that legal status is of particular significance in dealing with professional authoritative bodies or persons including medical practitioners, as the issue of parental responsibility would be central in determining who may and who cannot provide consent for the child's (non-emergency) medical treatment.[82] Hence, the absence of legal status accorded to Helen, the co-mother, is clearly problematic when faced with

---

79 Emphasis added.
80 Cussins (1998), p 55.
81 Children Act 1989, s 3.
82 See Montgomery (2003), pp 289–304.

the practical considerations of caring for a child. Furthermore, one cannot assume that an application for a joint residence order will necessarily be successful. Andrea and Louise, for example, were unsuccessful in their application for a joint residence order in 1998.[83] Therefore, while provisions to confer parental responsibility on co-mothers *exist*, a joint residence order is *neither an automatic nor a guaranteed* route to attaining formal legal status in relation to one's donor-conceived child.

More recently, however, there have been statutory[84] and judicial shifts towards recognising same-sex parenting.[85] In the recent case of *Re G (children) (shared residence order: parental responsibility)*,[86] on appeal a joint residence order was granted to a lesbian co-mother following the breakdown of her relationship with the donor-conceived children's mother. In his leading judgment in the Court of Appeal, Thorpe LJ made clear that he would not countenance the marginalisation of the co-mother in the children's lives in the future. He stated:

> I am in no doubt at all that . . . the children required firm measures to safeguard them from the *diminution in or loss of a vital side of family life* . . . The parental responsibility order was correctly identified by the CAFCASS officer as the appropriate safeguard. The judge's finding required a clear and strong message to the mother that she could not achieve the elimination of Miss W [co-mother], or even the reduction of Miss W *from the other parent in some undefined family connection.*[87]

Lord Justice Thorpe does not address Miss W as a parent *per se* at any point in the judgment, referring only to the law as it relates to 'absent parents' generically,[88] or, as above, to the mother as the 'other parent'.[89] Nevertheless, his comments clearly indicate a firm recognition of the co-mother's *parental* role in the children's lives. It is hoped that with the Civil Partnership Act 2004 now in force, the emergent judicial trend towards recognising same-sex partnerships (including parenting arrangements) will continue in this vein.

In addition, as noted above, s 4A(1) Children Act 1989, in force since 30 December 2005, now enables co-mothers to apply for parental responsibility where they have entered into a civil partnership with the child's mother. While this provision extends the remit of s 4 and facilitates parental responsibility for co-mothers in the absence of a joint residence order, it nevertheless ensures that

---

83 See Jones (2003; forthcoming 2007).
84 This was acknowledged by Thorpe LJ in *Re G* [2005] EWCA Civ 462, at para 7. Citing s 75(2) Civil Partnership Act 2004 (which, when enacted, will amend Children Act 1989 s 4A(1) (acquisition of parental responsibility by step-parent) to include applications by civil partners), he stated that this is 'an indication of a perceivable statutory trend towards the relaxation of the boundary originally set by section 4 [Children Act 1989]'.
85 See Baroness Hale in *Ghaidan v Mendoza* [2004] 2 WLR 113, paras 141–3.
86 [2005] EWCA Civ 462. Now see also *Re G (Children)* [2006] UKHL 43, on appeal from [2006] EWCA Civ 372.
87 Para 27, emphasis added.
88 Paras 25, 27.
89 Indeed, this issue is only addressed specifically with regard to noting the mother's evidence that 'Miss W should be viewed as an extended family member, not in a parental position', para 11. However, no further discussion of the mother's evidence was undertaken with regard to this point.

only those who adhere to the normative lesbian family, as legislated by the Civil Partnership Act 2004, can seek and be accorded this status. Thus, as Davina Cooper and Didi Herman warned in 1995: 'As some lesbians and gay men gain admittance into the status quo, familial ideology may be strengthened and others may be further marginalized.'[90] Therefore, those women who cannot or will not align themselves according to the norm of the 'good' lesbian co-mother will continue to be excluded under these provisions.[91] For these reasons, I suggest that legislative changes be introduced, as discussed further below.

Guardianship

> Part of me thinks that in the event of my death nobody would contest my partner's right to be, you know, the parent of the child.[92]

While all four lesbian couples interviewed mentioned the possible use of guardianship, with the exception of Andrea and Louise, none had put this in place. A child's legal mother can appoint the co-mother to be a guardian for the child in the event of her death.[93] With guardianship, one acquires parental responsibility, which Chris Barton and Gillian Douglas[94] point out is 'the closest a parent can come to a unilateral transfer of parental responsibility'. In the context of lesbian couples who conceive through the use of licensed donor insemination, guardianship would not take effect unless and until the legal mother dies,[95] as there is no legal father.[96] Therefore, in terms of providing legal status in relation to the donor-conceived child, it is limited to providing *possible future* rights and responsibilities. Furthermore, s 6(1)–(4) Children Act 1989 provides circumstances in which guardianship can be revoked. In addition, a court order can terminate guardianship.[97] Therefore, while a guardianship provision may provide solace for some lesbian couples with regard to the co-mothers' legal standing, it is limited. Unlike parental status, it is not automatic; it is not 'for life'; nor does it render the donor-conceived child a member of the guardian's family. Nevertheless, it remains the *only* legal provision which the child's legal mother can make in favour of the co-mother without any external (judicial or other) scrutiny.[98] However, I would suggest that this need not be so.

Status implications: The way forward?

To address the status issues raised in my interviewees' accounts, I will focus on the three questions posed in the introduction.

---

90 Cooper and Herman (1995), p 176.
91 See Diduck (1998).
92 Beverley, interviewee.
93 Children Act 1989, s 5(3).
94 Barton and Douglas (1995), p 100.
95 Children Act 1989, s 5(6)–(8).
96 HFEA 1990, s 28(6).
97 Children Act 1989, s 6(7).
98 Barton and Douglas (1995), p 100.

Does Anglo-Welsh family law have the necessary mechanisms for recognising the parental role of co-mothers?

As outlined in the introduction, the legal concept of parenthood is made up of a number of components. Principally, these are: the parental status of either 'mother' or 'father' as registered following the child's birth; the concurrent allocation of parental responsibility (subject to s 4 Children Act 1989); and an (almost) inalienable link between the child and parent, and the parent's wider family. The closest analogy to the parental role of the co-mother is that of the unmarried male partner of a woman who undertakes licensed donor insemination to conceive their child. In an unprecedented move, Anglo-Welsh law provides legal parenthood for such men in the absence of the traditional markers of this status: that is, a marital link with the mother or an assumed bio-genetic tie to the child.[99] As Franklin[100] notes, this provision illustrates the exercise of new powers of legal discourse to confer parenthood. Clearly, Anglo-Welsh legal discourse can, where considered necessary or desirable (for policy reasons, for example, matching children to fathers as outlined above), change the 'markers' it renders significant to the ascription of parenthood. Therefore, I would submit that legal parenthood already provides the necessary mechanisms to recognise co-mothers' parental roles, although clearly access to this status is currently denied to them. (The policy reasons for this exclusion are discussed in the following section.)

Is 'parenthood' considered an appropriate status to reflect the role of co-mothers?

This question is more problematic, because of the ongoing debate between legal commentators as to the relative weight to be attached to genetic parentage, the intention to parent, or the ongoing care provided for a child, when ascribing legal parenthood.[101] In the context of assisted reproductive technologies, the genetic and intention models of parenthood have dominated the discussion;[102] therefore I will focus on them. Put simply, if genetic ties determined legal parenthood, only persons with a genetic relationship with a particular child would be legally recognised as her parents.[103] Clearly, a co-mother would not be able to substantiate such a

---

99 HFEA 1990, s 28(3). Though the case of *X, Y and Z v UK* (1997) 24 EHRR 143 involving a transsexual social father indicates that one must legally be considered to be a *man* for s 28(3) HFEA 1990 to apply. However, Gender Recognition Act 2004 s 9(1) states that after a full gender recognition certificate is issued 'the person's gender becomes for all purposes the acquired gender.' Consequently, a female-to-male transsexual could in future be legally registered as the father of a donor-conceived child. However, as s 12 of the 2004 Act makes clear, issuing a gender recognition certificate does not alter the (pre-certificate) parental status of an individual.

100 Franklin (1993), outlined above.

101 Barton and Douglas (1995); Bainham, (1999); Bridge (1999); Johnson (1999); Jackson (2001) and Chapter 4 in this volume; Herring (2004); and Probert (2004).

102 Bainham (1999); Probert (2004).

103 Currently this would mean a maximum of two parents, although Johnson (1999) discusses future possible developments in assisted reproductive technologies that could increase this number.

link. Given the increasing significance ascribed to the child's right to know her genetic origins,[104] the focus on the genetic model is unsurprising. However, as Bainham[105] concedes, as this is not the model followed in Anglo-Welsh law, it is 'too late to change course now'. Hence, the co-mother's lack of genetic relationship to a donor-conceived child should not completely undermine her potential claim to legal parenthood.

Could the intention model provide a means for co-mothers to gain legal parenthood? As the name suggests, the intention model ascribes legal parenthood in favour of a person only where that person intends to be a parent.[106] It is not without its criticisms, particularly on the construction of 'intent' in circumstances where contraception may have failed, among other examples.[107] However, as Jonathan Herring[108] notes, in the context of assisted reproductive technologies, the intention to be (or in the case of sperm donors *not* to be) a parent is '*crucial*' to the determination of parenthood, although, as Rebecca Probert[109] points out, this intention 'has to be combined with some action to bring about a birth'.

For the purposes of legal recognition under s 28(3) HFEA 1990, the action required of an unmarried male partner is to undertake treatment 'together' with a woman at a licensed clinic.[110] A co-mother's actions in attending a clinic with her partner, as the lesbian couples I interviewed reported they did, do not differ from those of a male partner, yet no legal status follows from their intention and concurrent action.

Clearly, there are policy reasons for the absence of legal status accorded to these women. First, lesbian families conceived through donation do not promote 'the family' norm, hence there is little impetus (legislatively or judicially) to provide legal recognition in the absence of the traditional markers of parenthood. This clearly evidences Haimes's[111] argument regarding the social management of families that 'transgress' traditional or 'assumed' familial forms. However, the continued potency of 'the family' norm, notwithstanding the fact that a decreasing number of persons 'experience' this form of family, has been subject to sustained criticism by feminist legal commentators.[112] I would argue that it is poor justification for the continued discrimination of co-mothers on the basis of their gender and sexual orientation. Second, as Probert[113] notes, recognising the status of the co-mother on the child's birth certificate would prove problematic to the promotion of birth registration as a record of 'historical truth'. However, in light of the provisions of s 27 and s 28 HFEA 1990, it is difficult to sustain the argument that birth certificates record the 'truth' of a child's genetic parentage. Nevertheless this

---

104 Wallbank (2004).
105 Bainham (1999), p 44.
106 Barton and Douglas (1995).
107 Probert (2004), pp 284–5; Herring (2004), pp 328–9.
108 Herring (2004), p 328.
109 Probert (2004), p 285.
110 *Re D* [2005] UKHL 33; Sheldon (2005); Lind (2003).
111 Haimes (2002).
112 O'Donovan (1993); Diduck (1995, 2003).
113 Probert (2004), p 278.

policy issue could, as Probert[114] suggests, prove problematic judicially if one were to seek to challenge the current provisions on the basis of discrimination on the grounds of sexual orientation.[115] I submit that legal parenthood is an appropriate status for lesbian co-mothers, and that the policy considerations outlined above provide no basis for the continued discrimination against these women. Further, legal parenthood would validate that which they have been *doing* in their families, and more accurately reflect their commitments to their children and to the relationships they have constructed with their children. While judicial resistance to such a challenge to the status quo seems to be ebbing,[116] the extent of the requisite attendant changes and the need to ensure procedural fairness dictate that legislative changes would be necessary.

How might lesbian co-motherhood be accommodated under Anglo-Welsh law?

As the main focus of this chapter was the impact of the (lack of) legal ascription of parenthood for establishing familial status and kinship naming practices in lesbian and heterosexual families conceived by donation, there is insufficient scope to consider the proposed changes in detail. Rather, the following comments are intended to be illustrative of the legislative changes one might expect in order to provide co-mothers with access to the status of legal parenthood akin to that provided to unmarried social fathers when they undertake *licensed* donor insemination.[117] I will address three possible changes: birth registration; allocation of parental responsibility; and consent provisions at licensed clinics. I begin with the most controversial proposal – amendments to the registration of a child's birth.[118] Providing co-mothers with legal parenthood would necessitate changes to ensure that they could be registered as a parent on the child's birth certificate. The kinship terminology used could prove problematic given the lack of consensus on the appropriate term used to refer to 'co-mothers', as outlined in the introduction. Nevertheless, it is proposed that the terms 'parent' or 'co-parent' might prove least contentious, given the anecdotal evidence discussed earlier in the chapter.[119]

Changes to the allocation of parental responsibility could follow the recent model under s 111 Adoption and Children Act 2002, amending s 4 Children Act 1989 to provide automatic parental responsibility for unmarried fathers upon joint registration with the mother. As outlined above, lesbian couples have successfully applied for joint residence orders, thereby providing the co-mother with

---

114 *Ibid.*
115 *Per Ghaidan v Mendoza* [2004] UKHL 30, [2004] 3 All ER 411.
116 *Ibid*, and the decision in *Re G*, as discussed above.
117 Clearly, a number of women become co-mothers following self-insemination (Saffron, 1998), to whom the consent provisions would not apply. Class issues and the access policies of licensed clinics, which can act to frustrate lesbian women's use of licensed donor insemination, are salient considerations but fall outside the scope of this chapter: see Jones (2003, 2004).
118 Births and Deaths Registration Act 1953.
119 See also Adopted Children and Adoption Contact Registers Regulations 2005, SI 2005/924, Schedule 1.

parental responsibility for the duration of the order.[120] However, automatic allocation upon joint registration with the mother would remove discrimination on the basis of sexual orientation. Finally, to avoid any evidentiary issues with regard to the legal ascription of parenthood, co-mothers could be required to sign consent forms at licensed clinics to signal their intention to create a legal relationship with the donor-conceived child (as per Kate's and Sarah's account above). This approach is adopted in s 6A Artificial Conception Act 1985 of Western Australia for lesbian women in *de facto* relationships, and could arguably provide a model for Anglo-Welsh law to follow.[121]

Conclusion

This chapter has considered the legal ascription of parenthood in the context of licensed donor insemination and, in particular, the subjective impact of the current provisions on naming practices in British families conceived through donation. Anglo-Welsh legal discourse has (unsurprisingly) framed parenthood through a hetero-normative lens, whereby social fathers are matched to donor-conceived children while concurrently lesbian co-mothers are marginalised through a process of exclusion. This has caused difficulties in terms of their legal status as parents and of their subjective negotiations of their social status as parents, including their naming practices. It has been argued that the kinship terminology used within their families and at licensed clinics concurrently indicates the normative effects of, *and* the strategic resistance to, their lack of legal status. In particular, the democratic naming processes undertaken by the interviewees suggest that 'parenthood' can be a transgressive term, providing a readily identifiable status and relationship to the child, but also that, in some cases, 'parent' is still less than transformative because of the set of legal norms that obscure the possibility in law of co-*mothers*. In response to the limited and precarious legal recognition of co-mothers' parental roles through joint residence orders or guardianships provisions, in the concluding section, consideration was undertaken of possible ways of altering access to legal parenthood. Given the *symbolic* importance of the legal ascription of parenthood highlighted in *all* (lesbian and heterosexual) interviewees' accounts, access to this legal status is crucial, not only on grounds of equality and non-discrimination, but also because of the concurrent *practical* and subjective significance it has to family life and the day-to-day care of children.

Acknowledgments

I would like to extend my deepest gratitude to the women and men I interviewed, and to Lisa Saffron (and others who remain anonymous) for introductions made on my behalf during the research process. I would also like to thank Alison

---

120 Children Act 1989, s 12(2).
121 I am grateful to both Carol Smart and Lisa Young for alerting me to the Australian provisions.

Diduck, Katherine O'Donovan, Jonathan Montgomery, Leonora Onaran, and the participants at the Cavendish-sponsored contributors' workshop for their insightful observations. This chapter was also presented as a staff seminar at the School of Law, University of Southampton, and I am indebted to my colleagues for their comments and support. I am also grateful to Roger Errington for information pertaining to the adoption regulations; and to Maureen McNeil and Julie Wallbank for their remarks on an earlier version of this chapter. This research was funded by an ESRC PhD studentship (Ref: R00429834811).

References

Bainham, A (1999) 'Parentage, parenthood and parental responsibility: Subtle, elusive yet important distinctions', in Bainham, A, Day Sclater, S and Richards, M (eds) *What is a Parent? A Socio-Legal Analysis*, Oxford: Hart Publishing

Barton, C and Douglas, G (1995) *Law and Parenthood*, London: Butterworths

Blythe, E and Moore, R (2001) 'Involuntary childlessness and stigma', in Mason, T, Carlisle, C, Watkins, C and Whitehead, E (eds) *Stigma and Social Exclusion in Healthcare*, London: Routledge

Bridge, S (1999) 'Assisted reproduction and the legal definition of parentage', in Bainham, A, Day Sclater, S and Richards, M (eds) *What is a Parent? A Socio-Legal Analysis*, Oxford: Hart Publishing

Comeau, D (1999) 'Lesbian no biological mothering: Negotiating an (un)familiar existence', 1(2) *J of the Association for Research on Mothering* 44

Cooper, D and Herman, D (1995) 'Getting "the family right": Legislating heterosexuality in Britain, 1986–1991', in Herman, D and Stychin, C (eds) *Legal Inversions: Lesbians, Gay Men and the Politics of Law*, Philadelphia: Temple University Press

Cussins, C (1998) 'Quit snivelling, cryo-baby. We'll work out which one's your mama!', in Davis-Floyd, R and Dumit, J (eds) *Cyborg Babies from Techno-Sex to Techno Tots*, London: Routledge

Daniels, K and Taylor, R (1993) 'Secrecy and openness in donor insemination', 12(2) *Politics and the Life Sciences* 155

Day Sclater, S, Bainham, A and Richards, M (1999) 'Introduction', in Bainham, A, Day Sclater, S and Richards, M (eds) *What is a Parent? A Socio-Legal Analysis*, Oxford: Hart Publishing

Diduck, A (1995) 'The unmodified family: The Child Support Act and the construction of legal subjects', 22 *J of Law and Society* 527

Diduck, A (1998) 'In search of the feminist good mother', 7 *Social and Legal Studies* 129

Diduck, A (2003) *Law's Families*, London: LexisNexis Butterworths

Dunne, G (2000) 'Opting into motherhood: Lesbians blurring the boundaries and transforming the meaning of parenthood and kinship', 14(1) *Gender and Society* 11

Foucault, M (1980) *Power/Knowledge: Selected Interviews and Other Writings 1972–1977*, Gordon, C (trans), Brighton: Harvester Wheatsheaf

Franklin, S (1993) 'Making representations: The parliamentary debate on the Human Fertilisation and Embryology Act', in Edwards, J, Franklin, S, Hirsch, E, Price, F and Strathern, M (eds) *Technologies of Procreation Kinship in the Age of Assisted Conception*, London: Routledge

Gabb, J (1999) 'Imag(in)ing the queer lesbian family', 1(2) *J of the Association on Research in Mothering* 9

Golombok, S, Lycett, E, MacCallum, F, Jadva, V, Murray, C, Rust, J, Jenkins, J, Abdalla, H and Margara, R (2004) 'Parenting infants conceived by gamete donation', 18(3) *J of Family Psychology* 443

Golombok, S, Brewaeys, A, Cook, R, Giavazzi, M, Guerra, D, Mantovani, A, van Hall, E, Crosignany, P and Dexeus, S (1996) 'The European study of assisted reproduction families: Family functioning and child development', 11(10) *Human Reproduction* 2324

Haimes, E (1990) 'Recreating the family? Policy considerations relating to the "new" reproductive technologies', in McNeil, M, Varcoe, I and Yearley, S (eds) *The New Reproductive Technologies*, London: Macmillan Press

Haimes, E (2002) 'When transgression becomes transparent: Limiting family forms in assisted conception', 9(4) *J of Law and Medicine* 438

Hayden, C (1995) 'Gender, genetics and gen-eration: Reformulating biology in lesbian kinship', 10(1) *Cultural Anthropology* 41

Herring, J (2004) *Family Law*, London: Pearson Longman

HMSO (1984) *Report of the Committee of Inquiry into Human Fertilisation and Embryology*, Dame Mary Warnock (Chairman), Cmnd 9314

Hoggett, B (1993) *Parents and Children – The Law of Parental Responsibility*, 4th edn, London: Sweet and Maxwell

Human Fertilisation and Embryology Authority (2004) *Code of Practice*, 6th edn, London: Human Fertilisation and Embryology Authority

Jackson, E (2001) *Regulating Reproduction Law, Technology and Autonomy*, Oxford: Hart Publishing

Johnson, M (1999) 'A biomedical perspective on parenthood', in Bainham, A, Day Sclater, S and Richards, M (eds) *What is a Parent? A Socio-Legal Analysis*, Cambridge: Hart Publishing

Jones, C (forthcoming 2007) *Figuring 'the Family': Late Twentieth-Century Accounts of Lived Experience and Legal Discourse Around Licensed Donor Insemination in Britain*, Edwin Mellen Press

Jones, C (2005) 'Looking like a family: Negotiating bio-genetic continuity in

British lesbian families using licensed donor insemination', 8(2) *Sexualities* 221

Jones, C (2004) ' "Oh we don't do anything like that here": Single women and lesbian couples' negotiation of access to donor insemination at British clinics', paper presented at the SLSA conference, Glasgow

Jones, C (2003) 'Figuring "the family": Late twentieth-century accounts of lived experience and legal discourse around licensed donor insemination in Britain', unpublished PhD thesis, University of Lancaster

Kennedy, I and Grubb, A (1994) *Medical Law: Text with Materials*, 2nd edn, London: Butterworths

Lee, R and Morgan, D (2001) *Human Fertilisation and Embryology: Regulating the Reproductive Revolution*, London: Blackstone Press

Lind, C (2003) '*Re R (Paternity of IVF Baby)* – Unmarried paternity under the Human Fertilisation and Embryology Act 1990', 15(3) *Child and Family Law Quarterly* 327

Montgomery, J (2003) *Health Care Law*, 2nd edn, Oxford: Oxford University Press

Murray, C and Golobmok, S (2003) 'To tell or not to tell: The decision-making process of egg donation parents', 6 *Human Fertility* 89–95

New Zealand Law Commission (2005) *New Issues in Legal Parenthood*, Report 88

O'Donovan, K (1988) 'A right to know one's parentage?', 2 *International J of Law and the Family* 27

O'Donovan, K (1989) ' "What shall we tell the children?" Reflections on children's perspectives and the reproductive revolution', in Lee, R and Morgan, D (eds) *Birthrights Law and Ethics at the Beginnings of Life*, London: Routledge

O'Donovan, K (1993) *Family Law Matters*, London: Pluto

O'Donovan, K (1998) 'Who is the father? Access to information on genetic identity', in Douglas, G and Sebba, L (eds) *Children's Rights and Traditional Values*, Aldershot: Dartmouth

Pfeffer, N (1987) 'Artificial insemination, in vitro fertilisation and the stigma of infertility', in Stanworth, M (ed) *Reproductive Technologies: Gender, Motherhood and Medicine*, Cambridge: Polity Press

Probert, R (2004) 'Families, assisted reproduction and the law', 16(3) *Child and Family Law Quarterly* 273

Saffron, L (1994) *Challenging Conceptions – Planning a Family by Self-Insemination*, London: Cassell

Saffron, L (1996) *What About the Children? Sons and Daughters of Lesbian and Gay Parents Speak About Their Lives*, London: Cassell

Saffron, L (1998) *Challenging Conceptions: Planning a Family by Self-Insemination*, Bristol: Lisa Saffron

Saffron, L (2001) *It's a Family Affair*, London: Diva Books

Sheldon, S (2001) 'Unmarried fathers and parental responsibility: A case for reform?', 9(2) *Feminist Legal Studies* 93

Sheldon, S (2005) 'Fragmenting fatherhood: The regulation of reproductive technologies', 68(4) *Modern Law Review* 523

Smart, C (1987) ' "There is of course the distinction dictated by nature": Law and the problem of paternity', in Stanworth, M (ed) *Reproductive Technologies: Gender, Motherhood and Medicine*, Cambridge: Polity Press

Snowden, R and Mitchell, G (1981) *The Artificial Family: A Consideration of Artificial Insemination by Donor*, London: Allen and Unwin

Strathern, M (1992) *Reproducing the Future: Essays on Anthropology, Kinship and the New Reproductive Technologies*, Manchester: Manchester University Press

Thompson, C (2001) 'Strategic naturalizing: Kinship in an infertility clinic', in Franklin, S and McKinnon, S (eds) *Relative Values Reconfiguring Kinship Studies*, Durham, NC: Duke University Press

Wallbank, J (2001) *Challenging Motherhood(s)*, Essex: Pearson

Wallbank, J (2002) 'Clause 106 of the Adoption and Children Bill: Legislation for the "good father"?', 22(2) *Legal Studies* 276

Wallbank, J (2004) 'The role of rights and utility in instituting a child's right to know her genetic history', 13(2) *Social and Legal Studies* 245

Weeks, J, Heaphy, B and Donovan, C (2001) *Same Sex Intimacies: Families of Choice and Other Life Experiments*, London: Routledge

Chapter 6

After Birth: Decisions about Becoming a Mother
Katherine O'Donovan and Jill Marshall

Introduction

Debating the nature of autonomy is central to feminist theory. Taking control of one's own life is a foundation of feminism, and, strategically, autonomy is important to feminism as it allows for agency, change and self-determination. Feminism proposes ways of knowing and being in which a self is developed – a self that is not produced entirely by socialisation.

Yet contests over autonomy continue. On the one hand, social constructionism creates a deterministic account of preferences and a denial of agency. On the other hand, concepts of autonomy have been said to assume a freedom which does not exist for many women, or which may not exist at all, for *anyone*. Conceptions of autonomy may themselves be constructed, and also gendered. As Jennifer Nedelsky reflects, feminist theory has to hold on to autonomy, whilst arguing for a contextually situated self: 'The problem, of course is how to combine the claim of the constitutiveness of social relations with the value of self-determination.'[1] Holding both views simultaneously is the strategy that has been advocated by recent theorists,[2] and reconceiving autonomy is often stated to be the goal of such discussions.

Feminist theory entered a pessimistic period in the recent past. The attack on essentialism in the 1990s created difficulties in speaking generally about women.[3] Individual biographies are unique, it was said. Yet, as women, we do have common concerns, including our potential for childbearing and mothering during a stage of life, with their attendant social meanings in the societies in which we live. In response, some writers proposed a return to norms, particularly those in the form of rights.[4] But, as has been observed,[5] it is far from clear that this is the answer. As contests take place over, and between, rights, the problem of essentialism seems merely to be shifted to another scene.

Yet, for some second wave feminists, children are still central to arguments about autonomy. Debates over issues such as abortion, extra-uterine birth, work–life balance, bodily integrity, and making a life plan are, at their core, arguments about autonomy. This chapter explores themes of autonomy in the context of reproductive decisions but focuses upon choices to take up mothering after giving birth. Like Sarah Ruddick, we wish to separate birthing labour from mothering. Honouring 'both kinds of work and at the same time' providing 'the conceptual

---

1 Nedelsky (1989), p 221.
2 Jackson (2001); Nedelsky (1989).
3 See, for example, Malik, Chapter 11 in this volume.
4 For example, Nussbaum (2000).
5 Jackson and Lacey (2002).

and emotional space to raise questions about the relations between them', Ruddick argues that these labours do not necessarily have to be performed by the same mother.[6] Maternal work, undertaken in both forms of labour, might continue by the same woman after birthing, or might be transferred to others.

The recent case in the Court of Appeal of a woman who attempted to have her child adopted, having concealed her pregnancy from her husband and family, will be used as a reference point for discussions of separating 'mothering' activities from the legal and cultural structures surrounding giving birth.

Part One analyses the portrayal of women's choices in relation to bearing and rearing children in feminist literature. Although the literature is vast, the distinctions between pregnancy, childbirth and rearing children are often blurred and rarely made explicit. Part Two examines the decision to become a mother, drawing on ideas about autonomy and choice and the structural conditions within which such decisions are made. The distinction between deciding to continue a pregnancy, but not to take up mothering after giving birth, is important to this part. In Part Three, the legal position of women who wish to give birth anonymously or to place their infant for adoption in secret is examined. The recent decisions of the Court of Appeal on adoption of a child where pregnancy was concealed,[7] and of the European Court of Human Rights on anonymous birthing,[8] are explored.

Part One

This part of our paper focuses on what feminists have to say about women's autonomy, or lack of autonomy, in relation to their reproductive capacities and child-caring responsibilities. We begin by investigating the general feminist literature on women's ability to make choices and the concept of autonomy. We then move on to analyse the work of feminists who highlight what they describe as the 'natural' capacity of women to be child bearers and rearers. In our interpretation, these feminists argue that the only way for women to have autonomy is to overcome and transcend this capacity. We then consider the work of feminists who celebrate the 'natural' capacity of women as child bearers and rearers as providing women with a sense of human connection. Finally, we analyse those who critique the institution of motherhood as a patriarchal, socially constructed institution. Our analysis throughout is on whether, and if so, how, the literature makes a distinction between women's child-bearing and child-rearing capacities in the context of our ability to choose our own ways of life.

A primary theme in the feminist literature is analysis of the different spheres of public and private.[9] Women are said to be generally assigned to the latter – the domestic sphere of the home – which requires analysis of women as wives and

---

6   Ruddick (1989), pp 18–19. Ruddick's distinction has been made in French law since the eighteenth century.
7   *Re AB (Care Proceedings)* [2003] EWCA Civ 1842.
8   *Odievre v France* (Application no 42326/98) 13 February 2003; [2003] 1 FCR.
9   See O'Donovan (1985); Olsen (1995); Pateman (1987; 1988); Lacey (1998).

mothers in the family, rather than as autonomous persons in our own right.[10] This work highlights the political nature of the division, the perceived shortcomings of political systems, particularly liberalism, which it is claimed create and rely upon it, and the impact it has on women's lack of choices in ways of living their lives. These feminists critique the role motherhood plays in viewing women as somehow separate, meaning different or deviant, in comparison to 'normal' citizens, and they debate the meaning of, and role for, equality and an ethic of care in women's lives.[11]

Motherhood features prominently in each of these debates. An ideology of motherhood has played a part in women being seen as inferior to men, or at least as separate and distinct from them. This ideology of motherhood has an effect on women's autonomy, so that we are often not viewed as persons in our own right, with choices to make about ways of being and living.

Women's choices

While the idea of autonomy has increased in importance in many areas of law,[12] it has been subject to critique by many feminist theorists. Some have concluded that its meaning is, at worst, incomprehensible or, at best, of little value or use to feminism. At the same time, however, most agree that some idea of choice and freedom, autonomy if you like, is needed if women are to have any control over our own lives.

The idea of autonomy is most commonly associated with Immanuel Kant.[13] In Kantian autonomy, a person is capable of rational choice through exercising his or her own moral judgments governed by moral law. Many feminists have been critical of such a conception, as it is said to privilege male norms: rationality and reason being historically and conceptually associated with male ways of knowing and being and defined by the exclusion of the feminine.[14]

Other versions of autonomy see it as a way of being that is somehow independent of the context in which the individuals who exercise it are living. Accordingly, it has been presented as a quality of an independent, isolated, 'atomistic', 'unencumbered' individual.[15] Marxist and communitarian theorists have criticised this view and feminist critics have also done so. Some have observed, for example, that this 'atomistic' view of persons necessarily excludes women who are pregnant: the foetus is connected to them. Also, if women as mothers have responsibilities as the carers of dependent children, particularly if they are the sole carer, it is difficult to see how we can be described as autonomous in this sense: surely we will be constrained by dependants' reliance on us.

---

10 Okin (1979; 1989).
11 Du Bois (1985); Pateman (1987); Olsen (1995); Phillips (1999); MacKinnon (1989); Gilligan (1982); Bock and James (1992).
12 This is particularly the case in medical ethics.
13 Kant (1988); see also Dworkin (1999).
14 See Lloyd (1984).
15 Taylor (1992); Sandel (1998); see analysis also by Reece (2003), ch 2.

These observations mean either that pregnant women and mothers simply cannot be autonomous beings, or that the concept of autonomy must be revised to account for them. Indeed, more sophisticated versions of autonomy demonstrate that 'atomism' is unnecessary. In these versions, feminists have sought to reconceive autonomy, aiming to retain the indispensable notion to feminism that women should be free to make our own choices, while acknowledging the socially constructed quality of the choices people make.[16] In particular, certain feminists have been keen to stress the importance of relationships and interdependence in developing the capacity for autonomy, and have questioned what it is that enables people to be autonomous, in the sense of being free to make our own choices in life. They answer that autonomy is not concerned with isolation but depends upon the existence of relationships that provide support and guidance: relatedness is not the antithesis of autonomy but its precondition.[17]

So, autonomy is *all about* the ability to make choices and those choices are all about an individual's connectedness with, rather than its isolation from, other autonomous beings. Autonomy can thus be conceived of as a quality that develops and exists *because of* the interdependency of persons and encouragement of supportive others. As such, pregnancy and child rearing are not in conflict with the autonomy of any particular woman involved in such situations. Decisions to become pregnant, remain pregnant, become a mother on birth or not must all be viewed as exercises of choice by the particular women involved in those decisions. A view that presents these as situations that happen to women without any decision on our part can be criticised for hindering women's ability to live lives of our own choosing.

As much of the impetus for feminism and feminist politics arises from women claiming the space to choose who and what we are, to refuse to be defined, contained and dictated by notions of what society means by 'woman',[18] some conception of capacity for choice needs to be retained. But how is this best done, particularly in the context of pregnancy and child care? Various feminist theorists have considered this issue. In the next three subsections, we investigate their work and interpret it in the context of women becoming mothers.

Women as mothers – a natural phenomenon that must be overcome

Certain feminists have viewed women's capacity for motherhood as a natural, biological phenomenon, but one that thereby prevents women from being capable of living a fully autonomous life. These feminists require that women overcome their 'natural' state to become free and autonomous.

In existential feminist theory, becoming a woman is a socially constructed condition.[19] On this view, 'woman' is a creation, the 'other' to man: what women

---

16 Nedelsky (1989); MacKinnon (1989); Nussbaum, (1999; 2000); MacKenzie and Stoljar (2000).
17 Nedelsky (1989); MacKenzie and Stoljar (2000).
18 Phillips (1993), p 43.
19 De Beauvoir (1997); Lloyd (1984).

need to do, therefore, is to contest this construction, because it prevents us from living an autonomous and self-willed life, which is the ideal for everyone. Although it is acknowledged that a *completely* autonomous life is impossible, because as part of the human condition all persons are constrained by social and moral norms and bodily needs, individuals are still capable of constantly and deliberately taking responsibility for their obedience and disobedience to authority and to their bodies. To exercise what it is called 'authentic' choice, individuals must aim to transcend the social and the physical. For women, this means transcending female biology and instead entering into public life, engaging in our own projects and exploits. In such a presentation of becoming a woman, female biology is represented as conflicting with, and in opposition to, the ideal of the free autonomous subject reaching out to transcendence. Female biology and the female body drag this free autonomous subject back to a 'merely natural' existence: the female body is an intrinsic obstacle to transcendence and 'authentic' choice.

The achievement of autonomy for women thus comes by women actively choosing not to be immersed in their biology, including choosing not to become pregnant, not to have children and not to become mothers. What is proposed instead is a new order in which woman becomes part of the world of the active other; woman becomes like man in order to escape the debilitating and endlessly disempowering impact of femininity as the condition of otherness.[20]

However, in this type of feminist work, no distinctions are explicitly made between pregnancy and motherhood. Both of these conditions need to be refused. This work can be interpreted as identifying the choices necessary for autonomy in the social world as it now exists, but different choices might be required if the experience of a female body was not culturally objectified by exposure to the male gaze as it is now. In other words, if the world we live in was different, perhaps it would not be necessary to transcend female biology in the way proposed.

Certain radical feminist thinkers, particularly in the early second wave, reach similar conclusions about transcending female biology. Perhaps the starkest example of this type of work can be seen in Shulamith Firestone's *Dialectic of Sex*. In that analysis, the natural reproductive difference between the sexes is described as the first division of labour at the origins of class.[21] It is a natural, biologically based imbalance of power between men and women. However, given that individuals are no longer 'just' animals, they can oppose nature; they can take control of it. Given this state of affairs, humanity can outgrow nature, leading to the abolition of '*a discriminatory sex class system*' no longer justifiable on the grounds of its purported origins in nature.[22]

On this view, women will never be free of the constrictions of nature unless human reproduction becomes artificial reproduction in which children would be born to both sexes equally or independently of the other. Any dependence between

---

20 See Evans (1997), p 45.
21 Firestone (1971), pp 8–9.
22 Firestone (1971).

the child and the mother would give way to a greatly shortened dependence on a small group of others in general, 'freeing' women from their reproductive biology.

Again, no distinctions are made between the capacity to be a child bearer and a mother. Clear boundaries are drawn between child 'production' and subsequent development, but it is assumed that this can only happen if children are 'produced' separately from the natural reproductive and gestation process. It seems to be assumed that if women continued to be child bearers in the 'natural' way, we would be mothers simply by virtue of that.

Women as mothers – a natural phenomenon that must be celebrated

Other theorists present very different views of women as mothers. While the distinction between women and men continues to be based on our reproductive capacities, instead of this being negatively viewed as a hindrance to women's ability to live freely, it is instead seen as something to celebrate.[23]

In what has been called the 'unofficial story' of legal theory, as presented by cultural feminism, women are connected to others materially and existentially, in particular at four stages throughout our lives: menstruation; heterosexual penetrative sexual intercourse; pregnancy; and breast feeding.[24]

What is valued in the 'official story' of legal theory, however, is an autonomous individual who is separate from others, left alone to exercise voluntary choices in as many spheres as possible through the satisfaction of subjective desires and preferences. Even if maximisation of self-welfare as the motivation for actions is true of men, however, and some suggest that it is not, cultural feminism questions whether it is true for women. Moreover, cultural feminism is often less concerned to question the traditional masculine story of the isolated self than it is to revalue, in the public and the private spheres, the feminine relational self. On this account, because of the sense of connection felt by women, women's lives are not autonomous, they are 'profoundly relational': women cannot be autonomous separate individuals in a way which may be true of men. Because of this, the legal system and legal language fail women: they fail to represent or even comprehend women's sense of connection, fear of separation,[25] fear of lack of intimacy, experiences and what we view as harms.

Feminist analysis in this vein appears to make no distinction between the non-pregnant woman, the pregnant woman, the woman who gives birth, and the carer of the child. Women's moral voice is described as one of (potential) responsibility, duty and care for others, because our material circumstances involve responsibility, duty and care for those who are first physically attached, then physically dependent and then emotionally interdependent.[26]

---

23 Gilligan (1982); Rich (1976); West (1988).
24 West (1988).
25 According to West (1988), women fear separation from the other rather than annihilation by him, and count it as a harm, because women experience the separating pain of childbirth and feel more deeply the pain of the maturation and departure of adult children.
26 West (1988).

Often, in these feminist arguments, the mother–child relationship is presented as the essential human relationship; the family as constructed in patriarchy ruins this fundamental 'natural' human unit.[27] Proposals can then be made to abolish the patriarchal institution of motherhood, not motherhood itself, thus releasing what is described as 'the creation and sustenance of life into the same realm of decision, struggle, surprise, imagination and conscious intelligence as any other difficult but freely chosen work'.[28] Until then, however, so-called 'choices' facing women trying to be autonomous in a society which insists that we are destined primarily for reproduction, a choice presented as a mutually exclusive either/or between motherhood or individuation, motherhood or creativity, motherhood or freedom, are criticised.[29] On this feminist view, women's autonomy is *strengthened* through free exercise of their sexual and procreative choice, including choosing to become a mother, in conjunction with their claim to personhood. Women feel and are more autonomous through their own freedom to exercise their own choices in relation to maternity and motherhood; they are not to be used as a womb or a body part but to speak for themselves, in their own right.[30] In many ways, this view is similar to that presented by the next body of theorists we identify in the feminist literature: those feminists who see the structure of motherhood as patriarchal but remain more ambivalent as to the potential creativity and natural fulfilment that a more 'authentic' experience of motherhood can entail.

Women as mothers – institutional problems

Motherhood is presented in this literature as an institution or structure, usually constructed by patriarchy, in which women are portrayed as the natural carers of children. This motherhood is a socially constructed 'myth' perpetuating oppression and patriarchy, restricting women's equal opportunities[31] and constraining women's life plans.[32] On our review, this seems to be the most common approach in second wave feminists' analyses of motherhood. A common theme in the early feminist work was to stress the correlation between reproduction and production in a structural way.[33]

While acknowledging the obvious, that it is women (but not all women) who become pregnant and give birth, these feminists dispute the inevitable link that is then made to rearing children. These feminists aim for a future where, at the very least, some change to existing child-care arrangements will occur in the public and private spheres; where society, men and women share caring responsibilities;

---

27 Rich (1976), p 127.
28 *Ibid*, p 280.
29 *Ibid*, p 160.
30 *Ibid*, p xxii.
31 Okin (1979).
32 Cornell (1998).
33 Chodorow (1978); O'Brien (1981); Dally (1982).

and where there will correspondingly be some sort of flexibility of work and a fairer work–life balance for all.[34]

Much of this feminist work originated in the discipline of developmental psychology.[35] This research shows that as a female child grows, she develops her sense of identity as continuous with her caretaker's – usually, therefore, her mother's – while a young boy develops a sense of identity that is distinguished from his caretaker's. The reason for this is that, as the child grows older, he or she identifies with the same-sex parent, and parents reinforce this identification. The early experience of being cared for by a woman, therefore, produces a fundamental set of expectations concerning mothers' lack of separate interests from their infants and total concern for their infants' welfare.[36] Indeed, this work questions whether there is too much connection of the mother to her infant, resulting in a sense of loss of self or autonomy in the mother.

Questions are also raised by these feminists as to whether women turn to children for what is lacking in our own lives, and serve only to reinforce our lack of autonomy. If social structures existed that allowed women to carry out mean-ingful productive work, and to have emotionally satisfying adult relationships, it is claimed, we would be less likely to 'over invest' in our children.[37]

Even though these feminists are able to separate the biological requisites of maternity from the structural meaning given to motherhood, they still make no explicit distinction between women as child bearers and women as child rearers. It is still assumed that the first will result in the second, at least in some shared way.

A different feminist perspective, yet one that can be categorised in the same way, concentrates on the justice of the family structure. The family is analysed as a breeding ground for an unjust society: in its current patriarchal gendered form, it upholds and perpetuates the existing power imbalances in favour of men. Some feminists critique 'malestream' liberal theorists for failing to apply principles of liberal individualism to both men and women in families. It is argued that this is needed to aim for justice within the family, which would then filter into every area of life because of the family's importance as the sphere where children learn about justice and morality for themselves.[38] Distinctions are made between the mother and the child's carer, but not between mother and child bearer. Indeed, she is defined as mother because she is the child bearer, and motherhood is not seen as something women can refuse on giving birth.[39]

We see then that, while the feminist literature problematises and contextualises motherhood, it does not go as far as we would go in raising a distinction bet-ween maternity and motherhood. The balance of this chapter will explore that distinction and the consequent possibilities it would create for women to choose one status but not the other.

---

34 Pateman (1987); Phillips (1993); Okin (1989); Chodorow (1978).
35 Chodorow (1978).
36 *Ibid*, p 208.
37 *Ibid*, p 212.
38 Okin (1989); Nussbaum (2000).
39 Okin (1989).

Part Two: Becoming a mother

One account of autonomy developed by feminist theory is in relation to the abortion decision. Whether this decision is seen as based on a liberal notion of choice or on a post-liberal concept of the self, there has been little contest, within feminism, about justification, which is presented as a personal choice. While the history of abortion does provide a context for a contest by women to gain control over their own bodies,[40] so does the decision to refuse motherhood after giving birth, which still remains largely unexamined.

Women who go through pregnancy are generally assumed to want a child; for otherwise, why not terminate? Conventional language conflates maternity and motherhood, with health practitioners referring to the pregnant woman as a 'mother' throughout her pregnancy. Our contention is that conceptual clarity requires a distinction to be made between maternity and motherhood, notwithstanding the assumption made currently that continued gestation signifies an intention to take up mothering.[41] Yet, as we shall argue below, there is little space for other intentions. Surrogacy, where a different intention is agreed and proclaimed at an earlier stage, might be an exception, and the surrogate appears to have been accepted as a social identity.[42] But the identity of a woman 'who gave away her child' seems to be less acceptable now for unmarried women than it was historically.

Even in feminist literature, motherhood is not often presented as a choice to be exercised *after* giving birth. Various stories are told of motherhood – of natural instinct, of altruism or martyrdom, of self-interest – and unpicking these is difficult. Not only are individual childhood stories of mother subjective and particular, but suggestions of a woman's choices after giving birth touch on fears of abandonment and rejection. Notwithstanding the contextual quality of individual biographies, mother love is taken to be universal, timeless and the same in space and time. Yet, might it not be the case, as Ruddick suggests, that a

> corollary to the distinction between birthing labor and mothering, is that all mothers are 'adoptive.' To adopt is to commit oneself to protecting, nurturing, and training particular children. Even the most passionately loving birthgiver engages in a social adoptive act when she commits herself to sustain an infant in the world . . . The work of a birthgiver is not compromised if she carefully transfers to others the responsibility for the infant she has birthed.[43]

Ruddick is here suggesting that mother-care can consist of transferring the actual care to others.

A woman's previous history, the attitudes of others, life plans, including plans in relation to the child, and the birthgiver's present identity will affect attitudes to

---

40 Sheldon (1997).
41 Or a resignation, again based on a conflation of the two concepts, that there is little choice to do otherwise.
42 Stumpf (1986), pp 187–208.
43 Ruddick (1989), p 51.

birthing labour.[44] It is self-evident that birthing involves a separation of a shared physical identity which has continued throughout pregnancy, during which the foetus depends on the woman. After birth, the woman regains her body to herself. Notwithstanding a claim that 'the baby is not planted within the mother, but (is) flesh of her flesh, part of her',[45] and the obvious lack of physical independence of the foetus, it is not being suggested that the foetus is part of the woman's body. As MacKinnon observes:

> Physically no body part takes as much and contributes as little. The foetus does not exist to serve the woman as her body parts do. The relation is more the other way around; on the biological level, the foetus is more like a parasite than a part. The woman's physical relation to her foetus is expected to end and does; when it does, her body still has all its parts.[46]

Having endured the birthing trauma, the woman, in Ruddick's terms, can now decide whether or not to take up mothering in relation to the now physically separate infant with whom she once shared a physical identity.

> Identity, and with it the ability to engage in moral activity, is formed in specific cultural and historical situations, and thus it coincides with subjectivity, the ability to judge and to act. The self is not conceived as an entity but as the protagonist in a biography.[47]

Yet mothering and being a mother are laden with social and historical meanings and contests. As we saw, even in feminist theory, motherhood is seen as a source of both joy and oppression. Alison Diduck notes that relationships between parent and child 'are assumed to be based upon the irrationality of ever-enduring love or upon timeless and universally understood *duty*'. This she terms 'the romantic' ideal. She contrasts this with 'relations in the ideal modern family' that are said to be based upon 'choice, flux and freedom'.[48] Once mothering is taken up, a woman is faced with both imperatives. She is subjected to advice, comment, and criticism and, in advanced Western societies, to a highly demanding standard of knowledge of psychology, first aid and education. And through it all, maternal sacrifice, maternal instinct and empathy are expected of her.[49]

The ideology of motherhood, as analysed in popular American accounts, requires a level of devotion, self-abnegation and perfection that one might think sufficient to discourage mortal women.[50] Named the 'new momism', this ideology is diffused throughout the media, including on popular television shows, with the insistence 'that no woman is truly complete or fulfilled unless she has kids, that women remain the best primary caretakers of children, and that to be a remotely decent mother, a woman has to devote her entire physical, psychological

---

44 Sarah Ruddick (1989) includes the work of gestation and the trauma of giving birth in the idea of birthing labour.
45 Rothman (1989), p 161.
46 MacKinnon (1991), p 1316.
47 Sevenhuijsen (1998), p 56.
48 Diduck (2003), p 83.
49 Douglas and Michaels (2004).
50 See, eg, Crittenden (2001); Eyer (1996); Maushart (1999).

emotional, and intellectual being 24/7, to her children'.[51] 'Mom' is an identity, constructed for a market promoted in the media, containing a romanticised yet demanding view of what it means to mother. 'Mom' is a cultural icon whose standards of perfection are, in reality, unattainable.

Why might it be important to seek freedom for women to decide on whether or not to take up mothering after giving birth? Empirical research indicates that, aside from women who do not seek an abortion for personal reasons, or cannot do so because of legal prohibitions, some enter into a state of denial; others, aware of their pregnancy, cannot cope with the steps necessary to terminate.[52] Yet others choose motherhood as a positive step towards changing their lives.[53] It may be objected that teenagers who continue their pregnancies are 'non-copers', but the research shows that they exercise an element of choice.[54] A recent study of abortion decisions shows that young women from areas of social deprivation are more likely to become pregnant and are less likely to have an abortion than young women from more privileged backgrounds, who are less likely to become pregnant, but once they do, are more likely to terminate. How women view motherhood in their future lives is considered by the study as crucial to the outcome of conception. The evidence is that, where motherhood is seen as a positive change to a present way of life, pregnancy will continue, whereas 'those who are certain that future life will develop through education and employment tend to opt for abortion'.[55]

The above might seem to suggest that the only moment to exercise choice in relation to motherhood is the moment of confirmation of pregnancy. Those who enter into a state of denial, or fail to confront a decision on abortion, might be regarded as powerless and paralysed. Research on infanticide suggests that a proportion of cases can be explained in these terms.[56] However, those birthgivers who decide to refuse mothering after delivery may also be said to exercise choice. And that choice depends on many factors, including present identity, previous life experiences, and the conditions in which the subject finds herself, including social structures. This is not to say that conditions of discrimination, economic disadvantage and social powerlessness should be accepted, but rather to recognise that these may limit the possibilities within which a decision is made.

A second story, therefore, is of motherhood as a foundation of gender discrimination, both in terms of labour in gestation and delivery, and in caring for children.[57] This story is not about love of one's child, but is about structures in society. It is these structures which limit efforts to make parenting gender neutral, despite the language of gender neutrality. The introduction of norms and rights

---

51 Douglas and Michaels (2004), p 4.
52 Brockington (1996).
53 Lee *et al* (2004).
54 National Research Council (1987), p 27, cited in Lee *et al* (2004), p 1.
55 Lee *et al* (2004), p 21.
56 Concealment of pregnancy followed by infanticide is reported in all studies: see Brockington (1996).
57 Firestone (1971); Okin (1989).

discourse into this arena may create more problems than it solves. One senses that the debaters on gender power and parenting have retired exhausted.

Further, the decision not to take up mothering once one has given birth may be based on identity: a self unable to see a way to encompass childrearing at present. Not unlike the 'encumbered self'[58] – that is, a self claimed by inescapable duties – the 'refusing self' might be said to make a decision which is conditioned by the present and past aspects of her life.[59] These stories address hidden aspects of motherhood. It is quite possible to love one's child passionately and still kick against those social structures which relate parenting to gender. However, the romantic ideal creates social problems in the decision to renounce motherhood, and essentialist notions of womanhood contribute to a discourse of condemnation.

These essentialist notions survive even feminist accounts of the subject as an autonomous agent in charge of her own life. The decision to renounce motherhood, for example, is said to be 'inauthentic', the illegitimate result of social conditions that overwhelm and contradict the subject's self-identity. Little account is given to the possibility that internal and external factors may be liberating as well as constraining for some; an autonomous subject can make life plans, change her situation, and resist the conditions of oppression. Identity, in other words, does not float free of its context.

Moreover, recent feminist accounts of identity recognise that the self is composed of fragments, a web, or perhaps a patchwork, according to Morwenna Griffiths.[60] That self is depicted as varying according to time and space and as constrained in a myriad of ways. But despite constraints, it is an agent capable not only of action, but also of continual self-creation of identity. This self makes itself, but not in conditions of its own choosing. Griffiths is drawn to the notion of 'authenticity', where 'selves are in a process of becoming', selves are constructed, a self has agency. The construction and maintenance of self takes place with and through others in the face-to-face sense, and in the structural sense. The past leaves traces, even unconsciously on the future self. (In)authenticity therefore seems to be actions or decisions out of line with identity. This approach remains within the social constructionist tradition, despite an effort to marry it to autonomous agency.

'Authenticity', as used in this discourse, must be understood in relation to agency and becoming:

> To be authentic requires acting at one's own behest both at a feeling level and also at an intellectual, reflective one . . . authenticity has to be achieved and re-achieved. Each action changes the context and requires understanding if authenticity is to be retained. Simply acting on what you feel will not answer. Nor will acting on what you think. Both are required, and it is difficult to know which to emphasise at any stage. The re-introduction of the term 'autonomy' into the explanation may help to

---

58 Sandel (1998), p 19.
59 Reece (2003), ch 1.
60 Griffiths (1995).

clarify the idea: autonomy comes from agency which takes place within a context of becoming.[61]

Griffiths argues that 'the individual can only exist through the various communities of which she is a member and, indeed, is continually in a process of construction by those communities'.[62] The communities include the wider society and its political categories, including gender. The structures of power in the society in which the self finds itself affect decisions and choices. Although these structures are themselves changing, giving rise to a diffusion of power and to plurality, nevertheless they impact on the subject, as do her past experiences. Thus a constrained subject is to strive for authenticity in her actions. If this is an account of moving towards freedom, including freedom from gendered societal expectations, it engenders hope, but if it is an idea of the 'right decision', it may mask coercion.

Identity can thus be presented as a matter of choice, but also as created by choices. The subject of post-liberal theory, 'embedded and constituted by context',[63] is the product of her relationships and experience. Although the context varies, both personal characteristics and a self develop. Yet the characteristics of the individual self are central to the achievement of self-realisation leading to autonomy and freedom. It is this achievement that leads to 'authenticity', where actions and decisions fit with one's sense of self. However, some subjects may be divided against themselves because of social experiences and the social conditions of their lives. How then can such subjects be autonomous or make authentic decisions? Difficulties in identifying an autonomous subject are evident in recent debates amongst theorists. Creating a gendered relational subject associated with some versions of feminism[64] minimises the role of agency and autonomy, but has not proved to be the way forward. The requirement of a constant effort in seeking authenticity is open to criticism as unattainable. The subject may never reach that desirable state. She may reproach herself in her reflexivity. And in the meantime, practical decisions once taken may not be revocable on re-assessment.

The traditional ideal of mother and child, instinct and the 'natural' are probably close to a communitarian version of the self. The mother–child relationship is described as 'innate'. For some feminists, this is as constructed a relationship as any other. From the child's perspective, it is one of those relationships from which personal autonomy is constructed. But is it an exaggeration to suggest that feminist theory has been reluctant to question this romantic ideal? For decades within feminist theory, notions of the natural have been scrutinised, and the commitment to a social constructionist account of mother–child relations has been sustained alongside the valorisation of those relations.[65] But the 'romantic/duty' ideal still has purchase.

The conventional reaction to a woman who 'gives away' her child is one of

---

61 Griffiths (1995), p 179.
62 *Ibid*, p 93; see also Malik, Chapter 11 in this volume.
63 Reece (2003), p 14.
64 Gilligan (1982).
65 Badinter (1981).

distaste, even horror. Such an 'unwomanly' woman is more like the wicked stepmother of fairytales than a 'real woman'. Even those sympathetic to her plight may tell the woman that the decision to renounce motherhood after giving birth is a debilitating action. When it is said 'you will regret that later', or 'it is not natural', the message is that the self is divided against the self, that the proposed action is inauthentic. Yet, as the notion of authenticity is sought, it moves like mercury out of grasp.[66]

Part Three: The story of a refusing mother

This is the story told by the Court of Appeal[67] after the Family Division of the High Court had refused the applicant's plea that her birthgiving be confidential. The woman in question gave birth to a child, having concealed the pregnancy from her husband and two children. She gave the child into the care of the local authority after the birth and wanted no further contact. Her explanation was that she was raped after a night out with women friends; that her husband could not be the child's father, as he had undergone a vasectomy six years previously; and that no sexual intercourse had taken place with him at the relevant time.

The local authority applied for a care order prior to the placing of the child for adoption. As the woman wished to exclude her husband from knowledge of the proceedings, this became an issue before the High Court. The decision was that the husband should be joined to the proceedings. The rule, at common law and by statute, is that the husband of a woman who gives birth is presumed to be the father of the child.[68] There is space in the application of court rules on care proceedings for the exercise of discretion as to the parties to be joined. However, both the trial court and, subsequently, the Court of Appeal refused to exercise this discretion not to join the husband.[69] This case illustrates the gendered content given by courts to the status of marriage, but also the continuation of stereotypical assumptions about motherhood.

It is true that, had the court exercised discretion, this might be considered as tantamount to an acknowledgment that the husband was not the child's father. And in the instant case, the trial court was 'far from persuaded that the mother's account of all that [rape and relationship with the husband] was either truthful or accurate'. The judge said: 'I have no confidence that her purpose in giving

---

66 Reece (2003) argues that the search for authenticity, in following the right path in personal decisions, can be never-ending, and is an aspect of the therapeutic state. Eventually this search is coercive, as much so as the traditional rules it replaces.

67 *Re AB (Care Proceedings)* [2003] EWCA Civ 1842.

68 Children Act 1989, s 2. Since he was married to the mother, he has automatic parental responsibility. Nevertheless, the case suggests that a discretion does exist on the question of whether he is joined as a party.

69 In *Re J (Adoption: Contacting Father)*, Family Division 14/02/03, upon the woman's request, the father of a child placed for adoption was not contacted. In *Re M (Adoption: Rights of Natural Father)* [2001] 1 FLR 745, the father was not contacted as there was 'no established family life'. See also *Re M (Adoption: Rights of Natural Father)* [2001] FLJ 240. Where 'family life' is established the court will require that the father be contacted: *Re R (Adoption: Father's Involvement)* [2002] 1 FLR 302. In these cases the parties were unmarried.

evidence before me was to give an accurate, full and truthful account of the relevant events.'[70] The woman's statement of her fears of domestic violence was cursorily ignored, both at trial and on appeal.

The subject constructed in the Court of Appeal

There are several levels at which the court decisions above can be interrogated. On a technical level, the decisions of the social services and court authorities on how to proceed, and even on how to frame the questions, were not inevitable. The woman's placement of the infant for adoption could have been handled differently. However, it is the language used in the Court of Appeal and the image of the woman concerned, and of 'appropriate behaviour', that is of interest here.

Having disposed of the woman's plea for confidentiality in birthgiving, Thorpe LJ explained 'the consequences':

> There is a human tendency, which we all recognise, to escape the consequences of our errors and shames. The mental search for an escape route is necessarily ego-centric and often inspired by fantasies. The appellant's success in giving birth to her daughter without the knowledge of her husband and her other children is surprising, leaving aside any comments on her responsibility and candour.[71]

The 'responsible subject', it seems, will face up to her errors and shames and be caring rather than egocentric. Yet, when we examine this in terms of the woman's story, it may be that her idea of responsibility is to place her child for adoption in confidence. The choices constructed in liberal discourse are linked to responsibility, but views of the content of responsibility may differ.[72] Such views and decisions following therefrom may be conditioned by context and identity. If some form of self-determination is allowed to subjects, then the notion of choice posits various possibilities for decision. It seems, however, that 'wrong' or inauthentic choices may open a space for state intervention.[73] The trouble with the notion of 'wrong' is that the next questions are 'wrong for whom?' and 'by what standards?'

The concealment of the care and adoption proceedings, as wished for by the birthgiver, 'was never a realistic conception', according to the appeal judge who supported this observation with a reference to 'the responsibilities of public authority, the rights of the child, the rights of the husband and the rights of her other children'.[74] There was no reference to the rights of the woman herself. She is depicted as a fantasist, who has failed to encounter reality and truth. The outcome was that the husband 'must be served with the proceedings'. Realistic or not, the

---

70 As detailed in the appeal: *Re AB* [2003] EWCA Civ 1842.
71 *Re AB*, para 19.
72 McClain (1996).
73 Reece (2003). The writers of this chapter have debated this point. One argues that autonomy is not just about 'doing your own thing', and that people should be helped to make the right choices. The other argues that there may be a distinction between what seems to be 'right' at the time and what one sees as 'right' in later years. When under pressure, it is the present that has to be taken care of, not the future.
74 *Re AB*, para 19.

option of confidentiality, or 'concealment', is recognised in other jurisdictions of the European Union, a point which will be developed below.[75] In English law, however, the subject who has recently given birth has no right to ask for privacy.

The final note struck by the appeal judge is one of hope, or possibly fantasy:

> The local authority must provide professional support in breaking the news to the family and in managing its aftermath. I say 'must' because from the point of view of the child in the case everything turns on how that process is managed. Obviously a possibility is that the encounter with reality and truth will lead to an outcome very different from that which the mother suggested to the judge. A possible outcome is that this little girl may never need an adoptive placement and that is a possibility which needs to be explored as a matter of great urgency.[76]

In a sense, the court disposes of the issue by reference to the rights of others. We are not suggesting that the normative language of rights can always be validated in relation to anonymous birthgiving. As noted above, the rights of the child, husband and other children are relevant considerations and may have to be balanced against a right of privacy claimed by a woman. However, as one who has fulfilled the first part of birthing labour, in gestating and bringing a child safely forth, her preferences deserve more respect than that accorded by either court. Rights discourse often turns into discussions of priorities and proportionality, with 'a rhetorical reference to responsibility being set up in opposition to rights'.[77]

Giving birth is positioned in the United Kingdom as a public act. A new person enters the world, her arrival must be documented in a birth certificate, showing the name of the woman who gave birth, who is the legal mother, regardless of whether she is the genetic parent.[78] The only recourse of a birthgiver who does not want to be identified is to give birth in secret and to abandon the child, committing at least one crime.[79] Estimates of the frequency of such actions in England and Wales vary, but an educated guess is about one hundred a year.[80] Concealment of parturition from a husband or family does not necessarily involve concealment of identity from the child, who, if adopted will have access to her original birth certificate at the age of 18.[81] However, an abandoned child whose birthgiver disappears will not have the mother's name on the birth certificate. Most of the debate on abandonment has taken place around the question of the child's identity rights,[82] with little focus on the birthgiver, for the obvious reason that her identity is unknown. There remain a small number of European countries, however, where a different view prevails, as shown in a recent case before the European Court of Human Rights.[83]

---

75 Scheiwe (2003), p 144.
76 Thorpe LJ in *Re AB*.
77 McClain (1996).
78 Registration of Births Act, 1953, s 2; Human Fertilisation and Embryology Act 1991, s 27.
79 Offences Against the Person Act 1861, s 27.
80 Panter-Brick and Smith (2000).
81 Adoption and Children Act 2002, s 79.
82 O'Donovan (2000a), pp 73–86.
83 *Odievre v France* (2004) EHRR 43, [2003] 1 FCR 621.

Giving birth anonymously

France, Luxembourg and Italy continue an ancient tradition whereby a woman can enter a hospital; give her name as X, indicating that she does not wish to reveal her identity; give birth; and leave her child in the hands of the authorities.[84] In *Odievre v France*,[85] the European Court of Human Rights, by a majority of ten to seven, upheld the provisions of the French Civil Code which enable anonymous birthing. Although the issue in that case is presented in terms of a right of access to information about one's origins, it can be represented as a case concerned with the autonomy of the birthgiver. It is estimated that a current 400,000 French persons were born to anonymous mothers.[86] Pressure groups exist to change the French legislation, but, whilst it has been modified, the woman's right has been maintained. The history of the French legislation has been documented elsewhere.[87] The focus here is on the construction of this right in the language of autonomy.

One approach to autonomy might argue that a woman who carries a child to full term and gives birth is not autonomous, for she is encumbered, confined, and analogous to the person portrayed in communitarian classics.[88] Even if this argument is acknowledged, it does not preclude the recovery of autonomy once confinement is over. In the French discourse of *accouchement sous X*, giving birth anonymously is positioned as a woman's right.[89] This position was upheld by the European Court of Human Rights, although the rationale for the decision was more in terms of welfare than autonomy.

In the judgment of the majority of the Court, various interests had to be weighed. Article 8 of the European Convention on Human Rights has been interpreted to cover identity rights. The interests of the applicant, now an adult, in knowing her origins and the identity of her biological mother are placed against the interests of the birthgiver, 'in remaining anonymous in order to protect her health by giving birth in appropriate medical conditions'.[90] Further considerations are the general interest of protection of health of both child and birthgiver and the avoidance of abandonment of a child at birth. These interests are presented as the right to life under Article 2 of the Convention. The Court observed that the competing interests between applicant and her biological mother 'do not concern an adult and a child, but two adults, each endowed with her own free will'.[91] This is the only suggestion of autonomy. It is noteworthy that, in justifying the decision, the right to life is trump, with welfare and health as the best suit.

Criticisms of the judgment are based on the identity rights of the child,

---

84 O'Donovan (2000b), pp 68–85.
85 *Odievre v France* (2004) EHRR 43, [2003] 1 FCR 621.
86 Steiner (2003).
87 O'Donovan (2000b). See also paras 15 and 16 of the judgment in *Odievre v France*.
88 Etzioni (1988). See also analysis in Part One above.
89 O'Donovan (2002).
90 *Odievre v France*.
91 *Odievre v France*, para 44.

recognised by international conventions, and come largely from France.[92] Other jurisdictions, such as Belgium and Hungary, provide a way for mothers to give birth *discreetly*. Some German Lander have already instituted baby boxes, where babies can be left anonymously, and legislation allowing anonymous births is under active consideration.[93] The language of justification in these jurisdictions is of protection of the life and development of the child. Thus, despite a growing trend in giving birth *discreetly*, it is only in France, Italy and Luxembourg that the political justification for anonymous birthing is couched in terms of women's rights. Steiner comments on this: 'One has to place the French legislation relating to anonymous birth in the wider context of parenthood, a concept in French family law at the heart of which has always existed an adult-centred individualistic philosophy of freedom of choice.'[94] To a degree, the concept of parenthood in French law is a question of volition.

Examination of the French discourse surrounding *accouchement sous X* reveals a variety of arguments. Although the antiquity of the woman's right involved goes back to the French Revolution, utilitarian arguments based on welfare and vulnerability and the characteristics of the women concerned are also used. Against the child's identity rights, the right to life is positioned as trumps. Yet beneath these arguments lie legal and cultural attitudes to the mother–child dyad.

Could it be that becoming a mother in the new century requires a different form of self-abnegation from that of the past? This is the thesis that is advanced in popular literature from the United States:

> Central to the new momism, in fact, is the feminist insistence that women have choices, that they have autonomy. But here's where the distortion of feminism occurs. The only truly enlightened choice to make as a woman, the one that proves, first, that you are a 'real woman', and second that you are a decent worthy one, is to become a 'mom'. Thus the new momism is deeply contradictory. It both draws from and repudiates feminism.[95]

Conclusion

Arguments about the self seem to turn into arguments about liberalism, agency and autonomy. Although liberalism may stand accused of denying 'the centrality of relationships in constituting the self',[96] an emphasis on each person as deserving equal concern and being of equal worth is valuable. This includes regarding women as of worth in themselves, rather than as reproducers and care givers. The trick is said to be to hold respect for choices alongside a web of connections that have moulded identity.

---

92 United Nations Convention on the Rights of the Child, Articles 7 and 8; European Convention on Human Rights, Article 8; Steiner (2003).
93 Scheiwe (2003). The situation in the United States, where anonymous abandonment has been legalised in a large number of states, is discussed in Magnusen (2001) and in Raum and Skaare (2000).
94 Steiner (2003), p 430.
95 Douglas and Michaels (2004).
96 Nedelsky (1989), p 221.

As feminists, we can fight against specific events, such as rape or abuse, and against structural conditions in the economy and social provisions that lead a woman to give up her child. But do we want to deny her the choice to do so? She may be making the best decision she can, for herself and her child. To stigmatise such a woman is wrong. Much of the post-liberal literature, with its emphasis on authenticity, suggests that choices are conditioned by socialisation, and that decisions can be inauthentic. We must be careful that such language does not hide coercion and a stereotypical idea of what it means to be a woman. Losing our analysis of the coercive nature of structures that limit lives has left feminist analysis at the mercy of the twin peaks of 'autonomy', as fleeting and only rarely exercised,[97] and socialisation, as restricting or even eliminating self-determination. Feminists must continue to fight for women's freedom to be and to become. In the meantime, recognition that decisions about motherhood are made within structures and constraints, both diffuse and direct, should not lead us to deny the ability to make them.

References

Badinter, E (1981) *Mother Love: Myth and Reality*, New York: Macmillan

Bock, G and James, S (1992) *Beyond Equality and Difference: Citizenship, Feminist Politics and Female Subjectivity*, London: Routledge

Brockington, I (1996) *Motherhood and Mental Health*, Oxford: Oxford University Press

Chodorow, N (1978) *The Reproduction of Mothering: Psychoanalysis and the Sociology of Gender*, Berkeley, CA: University of California Press

Cornell, D (1998) *At the Heart of Freedom: Feminism, Sex and Equality*, Princeton, NJ: Princeton University Press

Crittenden, A (2001) *The Price of Motherhood*, New York: Metropolitan Books

Dally, A (1982) *Inventing Motherhood: the Consequences of an Ideal*, London: Burnett Books

De Beauvoir, S (1997) *The Second Sex*, London: Jonathan Cape, 1953, Vintage

Diduck, A (2003) *Law's Families*, UK: LexisNexis

Douglas, S and Michaels, M (2004) *The Mommy Myth: The Idealization of Motherhood and How it Has Undermined Women*, New York: Free Press

Du Bois, E *et al* (conversants) (1985) 'Feminist discourse, moral values, and the law – a conversation', 1984 James McCormick Mitchell Lecture, 34 *Buffalo Law Review* 11

Dworkin, G (1999) *The Theory and Practice of Autonomy*, Cambridge: Cambridge University Press

---

97 *Ibid*, p 225.

Etzioni, A (ed) (1988) *The Essential Communitarian Reader*, Oxford: Rowman and Littlefield

Evans, M (1997) *Introducing Contemporary Feminist Thought*, Cambridge: Polity Press

Eyer, D (1996) *Motherguilt*, New York: Times Books

Firestone, S (1971) *The Dialectic of Sex: The Case for Feminist Revolution*, New York: Bantham Books

Gilligan, C (1982) *In a Different Voice: Psychological Theory and Women's Development*, London: Harvard University Press

Griffiths, M (1995) *Feminisms and the Self: The Web of Identity*, London: Routledge

Jackson, E (2001) *Regulating Reproduction: Law, Technology and Autonomy*, Oxford: Hart

Jackson, E and Lacey, N (2002) 'Introduction to feminist legal theory', in Penner, Schiff and Nobles (eds) *Jurisprudence and Legal Theory: Commentary and Materials*, London: Butterworths LexisNexis

Kant, I (1988) *Fundamental Principles of the Metaphysic of Morals*, New York: Prometheus Books

Lacey, N (1998) *Unspeakable Subjects: Feminist Essays in Legal and Social Theory*, Oxford: Hart Publishing

Lee, E, Clements, S, Ingham, R and Stone, N (2004) *A Matter of Choice?*, York: Joseph Rowntree Foundation

Lloyd, G (1984) *The Man of Reason: Male and Female in Western Philosophy*, London: Methuen

MacKenzie, C and Stoljar, N (eds) (2000) *Relational Autonomy: Feminist Perspectives on Autonomy, Agency and the Social Self*, Oxford: Oxford University Press

MacKinnon, C (1989) *Toward a Feminist Theory of the State*, London: Harvard University Press

MacKinnon, C (1991) 'Reflections on sex equality under the law', 100 *Yale LJ* 1281

Magnusen, D (2001) 'From dumpster to delivery room', 22 *J of Juvenile Law* 1

Maushart, S (1999) *The Mask of Motherhood*, New York: The New Press

McClain, L (1996) ' "Irresponsible" reproduction', 47 *Hastings LJ* 339

Nedelsky, J (1989) 'Preconceiving autonomy: Sources, thoughts and possibilities', in Hutchinson, A and Green, L (eds) *Law and the Community: The End of Individualism?* Toronto: Carswell

Nussbaum, M (1999) *Sex and Social Justice*, Oxford: Oxford University Press

Nussbaum, M (2000) *Women and Human Development*, Cambridge: Cambridge University Press

O'Brien, M (1981) *The Politics of Reproduction*, London: Routledge

O'Donovan, K (1985) *Sexual Divisions in the Law*, London: Weidenfeld & Nicholson

O'Donovan, K (2000a) 'Interpretations of children's identity rights', in Bridgeman, J and Monk, D (eds) *Feminist Perspectives on Child Care Law*, London: Cavendish

O'Donovan, K (2000b) '*Enfants trouvés*, anonymous mothers and children's identity rights', in O'Donovan, K and Rubin, G (eds) *Human Rights and Legal History*, Oxford: Oxford University Press

O'Donovan, K (2002) ' "Real" mothers for abandoned children', 36 *Law and Society Review* 347–78

Okin, SM (1979) *Women in Western Political Thought*, Princeton, NJ: Princeton University Press

Okin, SM (1989) *Justice, Gender and the Family*, New York: Basic Books

Olsen, F (1995) 'The family and the market', in Olsen, F (ed) *Feminist Legal Theory* (Vols 1 and 2), London: Dartmouth

Panter Brick, C and Smith, M (2000) *Abandoned Children*, Cambridge: Cambridge University Press

Pateman, C (1987) 'Feminist critiques of the public/private dichotomy', in Phillips, A (ed) *Feminism and Equality*, Oxford: Basil Blackwell

Pateman, C (1988) *The Sexual Contract*, Cambridge: Polity Press

Phillips, A (1993) *Democracy and Difference*, Cambridge: Polity Press

Phillips, A (1999) *Which Equalities Matter?* Cambridge: Polity Press

Raum, M and Skaare, J (2000) 'Encouraging abandonment', 76 *Notre Dame Law Review*

Reece, H (2003) *Divorcing Responsibly*, Oxford: Hart

Rich, A (1976) *Of Woman Born*, London: Virago

Rothman, BK (1989) *Recreating Motherhood: Ideology and Technology in a Patriarchal Society*, New York: WW Norton & Company

Ruddick, S (1989) *Maternal Thinking*, New York: Ballantine Books

Sandel, M (1982/1998) *Liberalism and the Limits of Justice*, Cambridge: Cambridge University Press

Scheiwe, K (2003) 'Giving birth anonymously – a suitable export from France to Germany', *International Family LJ* 144

Sevenhuijsen, S (1998) *Citizenship and the Ethics of Care*, London: Routledge

Sheldon, S (1997) *Beyond Control: Medical Power, Women and Abortion Law*, London: Pluto Press

Steiner, E (2003) '*Odievre v France* – desperately seeking mother – anonymous births in the European Court of Human Rights', 15 *Child and Family Law Quarterly* 425

Stumpf, A (1986) 'Redefining: A legal matrix for new reproductive technologies', 96 *Yale LJ* 187

Taylor, C (1992) 'Atomism', in Avineri, S and De-Shalit, A (eds) *Communitarianism and Individualism*, Oxford: Oxford University Press

West, R (1988) 'Jurisprudence and gender', 55 *University of Chicago Law Review* 1

Chapter 7

The Ethic of Justice Strikes Back: Changing Narratives of Fatherhood
Carol Smart

Introduction

In this chapter, I shall explore a number of themes which have come together to form the background to the re-ignition of a major gender struggle in the area of family life and family law. This struggle is ostensibly over children and, in particular, over how children's lives should be lived after the separation or divorce of their parents. However, I shall suggest that it is also a struggle to refashion and reposition fatherhood in the legal and cultural imaginary and that this has important implications for motherhood. My title, 'the ethic of justice strikes back', is, of course, a reference to the name of a relatively new fathers' rights group called Fathers4Justice, who have attracted a lot of media attention in the UK and who are influencing the direction of policy on matters of residence, contact and the relative standing of mothers and fathers in family law. The fact that they have claimed the term 'Justice' is significant, because English family law is not much concerned with justice as such and this group clearly identifies this term as one that can both reveal the injustices in the system, while also using a powerful political and moral rhetoric. But my title is about the ethic of justice and not simply the terminology of justice itself. I have chosen this formulation (in a semi-ironic fashion) because I wanted to think about whether ethical claims framed around justice still have a more powerful impact and a stronger moral imperative than claims based on care. So I became interested in the ways in which the moral hierarchy of claims within family law might be being reversed by the renewed call for justice. By this I mean that, in recent decades, English family law has been more concerned about the welfare of children, and also the importance of caring relationships, than it has been about justice or equality between spouses or adults. But clearly this can be reversed, and I began to speculate on whether the emergence of a group like Fathers4Justice could be the catalyst for just such a turnaround. However, the closer I looked at contemporary developments, the more I realised that, although the fathers' movement uses claims to justice, it also situates itself (rhetorically at least) within moral claims based on care. Now, I am not concerned with whether they *really* do employ an ethic of justice or an ethic of care in their practice; rather I am interested in how, in a popularised form, claims based both on justice and on care are being used and interwoven to create a specific narrative of fatherhood.

The themes I shall draw upon therefore include the political purchase of claims based on the ethic of justice versus the ethic of care; the difficulty of giving voice to the experience of motherhood when mothers are assumed already to be over-privileged; and the influence of new narratives of fatherhood, which are being articulated in the sphere of family law. None of these interrelated issues are new, but they come together at an important social and cultural moment to 'lock' together to form the basis of a new inferential framework within which gender relations are being redefined. I shall first look briefly at the now-familiar debate about the ethic of justice and the ethic of care to indicate why it is important to revisit some of these issues. I shall then, even more briefly, refer to the silence surrounding motherhood in the current discursive struggle and the rise of narratives of fatherhood (particularly in form of justice and rights), before turning to the substance of the chapter, in which I seek to pursue and articulate these points through the analysis of a key case on paternity and parental responsibility and selected interview data.

The ethic of justice and the ethic of care – again

The first issue which needs some clarification is the relevance here of the framework of the ethic of justice and the ethic of care, some twenty years after the work of Carol Gilligan was first published and after much has been published which further refines and develops these ideas.[1] It might be thought that enough has been said on these ideas, and indeed this point might have some validity. But I am not going to take these concepts forward as if they can throw yet more light on issues of gender and care; rather I want to treat them as narrative devices, which have themselves become part of the social relations which need to be analysed. So, from being a framework of analysis, I am suggesting that it is the deployment of the language of an ethic of justice or an ethic of care that now needs analysis. We need, for example, to understand the way in which a changing cultural and political context can transform the idea of an ethic of care from a potentially progressive concept into a new form of governance over family life. The unintended elision between the original feminist emphasis on the (unrecognised) care work and attentiveness of women (mothers in particular) and the rise of New Labour with its emphasis on ethical self-governance[2] and its requirement that parents must act ethically and responsibly towards their children has created a wholly new set of consequences for the articulation of an ethic of care. No longer can the ethic of care be seen as a feminist corrective to the influence of the ethic of justice (to simplify the argument somewhat), when the selfless pursuit of care and caring has become a governmental expectation within family policy. Feminist work on the ethic of care was never intended to be normative; rather, it was seen as a way to introduce values already held by individuals, but which were ignored or denigrated, into the public and legal domain. However, the responsibility to care (and to care responsibly) has become a part of family policy, so that what was an attempt to introduce everyday values into policy has found itself co-existing alongside a top-down imposition of values which appear on the surface to be broadly similar. As Gillies argues, 'reasonable, rational, moral citizens, by New Labour definition, seek to do the best for their children, and according to policy doctrine, government should play an active role in guiding and supporting them to

---

1   Gilligan (1982); Sevenhuijsen (1998); Tronto (1993).
2   Gillies (2005).

do so'.[3] Issues about caring properly are therefore part of the mainstream political agenda, but this does not mean that the agenda is now a feminist one in the way that authors like Tronto or Sevenhuijsen would recognise it. Of course, this kind of distorted co-option is not a new phenomenon, but it does have the tendency to rob a potentially critical or radical set of concepts of their political purchase.

At a more commonplace level within family law, I am, of course, aware that there has been a long-term conflict between ideals of justice and the protection of vulnerable members of families. Thus the notion of welfare has challenged (throughout the twentieth century at least) the former strict doctrine of rights, ownership and entitlement in family matters. While this debate has been referred to in terms of rights v welfare,[4] it is now important to broaden this conceptualisation away from a dualistic model (in which rights and welfare struggle against one another), in order to include the dimension of care, which is not reducible to welfare. We need to understand that there is now a three-cornered debate ongoing between 'rights talk', 'welfare talk' and 'care talk'. I am emphasising these styles of narration rather than the actual people doing the talking because I want to make it clear that these structures are available to mothers or fathers or lawyers or mediators or the Children and Family Court Advisory and Support Service (CAFCASS) officers or even children. The extent to which any one of these actors may deploy these narratives will vary, but the point I wish to make is that it would be a mistake to assume, for example, that fathers speak only of rights and mothers only of care or welfare. Actors can deploy more than one of these narrative styles, or can slip and slide between them. However, the impact of the deployment will vary according to such factors as gender, status, generation and so on.

It is perhaps necessary to define what I mean by 'rights talk', 'welfare talk' and 'care talk' and to say a few words on why I think we need the third element, that is, 'care talk', rather than remaining with a rights v welfare formulation. By 'rights talk', I mean those claims which can be made in relation to the state or in relation to another individual for recognition of entitlement. To frame a demand in terms of rights is a way of seeking a legitimating response and follows fairly clear steps or procedures. 'Welfare talk', on the other hand, derives from the philanthropic concern for those who are more vulnerable or in need of protection – possibly against those who have rights but who do not exercise their responsibilities appropriately. Although welfare talk derives from philanthropic interventions, it has been taken up and used by individuals in disputes and is not the sole narrational prerogative of social workers, expert witnesses and others in formal or quasi-formal positions within family law. In other words, anyone may now deploy the terminology of 'the welfare of the child' in disputes in family law. Moreover, as is well established, what constitutes 'welfare' (or the best interests of the child) is a contested and constantly moving and redefinable notion.[5] 'Care talk' should not be confused with 'welfare talk'. Following Tronto,[6] we can see that 'care talk' may

---

3   Gillies (2005), p 77.
4   Murch (1980); James and Hay (1993).
5   Smart and Sevenhuijsen (1989); Diduck (2003).
6   Tronto (1993).

involve speech about practical aspects of caring for others (in this context, children) or talk about how much parents care about their children. 'Care talk' may have virtually no overlap with 'welfare talk', while it may even, in some contexts, be deployed to support 'rights talk'. So, for example, a father may base his rights claim (for example, to a 50:50 share of his child's time) on the basis that he asserts how much he cares for and about his child. By comparison, a mother may resist the claims deriving from the father's 'rights talk' and from the court's 'welfare talk' by asserting her care for and about the child, which gives her a prior and superior understanding of the situation.

Thus it is important to recognise that the argument which follows is attempting to draw particular feminist insights into the current struggle between motherhood and fatherhood, but I am not using the idea of an ethic of care uncritically, nor am I offering an essentialist argument, which suggests that only fathers use the register of 'rights talk' and only mothers engage in 'care talk'. Rather, there is a subtle interplay of all these forms and what may be occurring is a shift in the balance of the influence of these claims. I shall argue that if fathers made claims solely in terms of rights they would make little headway, but because their rights claims are based on care talk and because, at this particular cultural moment, fathers are redefined as central to children's welfare,[7] fathers' definitions of gender relations in families are in the ascendant.

The exclusion of motherhood from the debate

A new 'truth' appears to have been established in which all debates about children and residence after divorce or separation are premised on the assumption that courts favour mothers over fathers.[8] This 'injustice' is treated as self-evident[9] because, statistically, after divorce or separation, children are still far more likely to live with their mothers than with their fathers.[10] In the face of such an apparently incontrovertible 'truth', it is hard to compose a counter-argument which does not appear to be denying fathers their 'rights' or to be asserting that fathers cannot or should not care for their children. Mothers have thus become defined as an obstacle to justice for fathers and, to a lesser extent, as obstacles to their children's welfare if they (appear to) fail to recognise the importance of care provided by fathers.[11] Alternative arguments are defined as partial because of the highly polarised nature of the current debate. Moreover, they are seen as antithetical to fairness and ultimately as neglectful of the proper welfare of children. Themes which once

---

7 Advisory Board on Family Law (2002); Amato and Booth (1997); Morgan (1998).
8 See also Kaganas, Chapter 8 in this volume.
9 For example, the headline in *Guardian Unlimited*, 28 October 2004, read 'Stand up for your rights, minister tells fathers'. The minister was Lord Filkin, who has responsibility for reform of existing policies in family law. Also John Humphreys, on the BBC Radio 4 programme *Today*, 18 June 2004, stated that we all know that fathers are discriminated against.
10 Smart *et al* (2003).
11 Wallbank (1998).

spoke of the significance of the 'primary carer', for example,[12] or which construct the field of parenting and caring outside the framework of 'equality' have become virtually unspeakable, and certainly suspect within family law discourses. This is because the 'care talk' of mothers engaged in contact or residence disputes is treated either as unremarkable (it is mothers' duty to care, so this does not constitute a special claim), or as simply insignificant when compared with the combined 'rights talk' plus 'welfare talk' plus 'care talk' of the fathers' rights movement. This means that there is no way that motherhood can be legitimately positioned in the debate, notwithstanding the fact that mothers are still the primary carers of children. Moreover, because in the wider policy context 'responsible caring' has become a doctrine of good parenting, any behaviour which seems to deviate from this model is seen as requiring correction. It is mothers, therefore, who are seen to be in need of remedial intervention;[13] or, as Gillies has framed it, it is predominantly mothers who are now required to practise ethical self-governance.[14]

Narratives of fatherhood

When considering the significance of demands for equality and justice for fathers on divorce, it is important to recognise that groups such as Families Need Fathers or Fathers4Justice were forged out of a sense of loss of privilege and in competition with mothers, whom they defined as being too powerful in matters to do with children.[15] The focus on fatherhood at the time of divorce has pushed these groups into a very combative style, which seeks to harness much of the pain associated with separation into a focused anger[16] around claims to children.[17] But the movement is not simply about claiming equal rights over children on divorce or separation; it is also about making new kinds of claims to children and hence to fatherhood. This means that, although there is a specificity about their claims (for example, for 50:50 sharing of children), they are a catalyst for wider demands which are taking new forms (as discussed below), which in turn extend the scope of fatherhood and also, by definition, start to redefine motherhood. This suggests that the new articulation of the meaning of fatherhood, which is now given voice through the pursuit of legal claims, is more than the voicing of a pre-existing but silent claim, but is actually part of a new discursive construction of fatherhood.

The success of pressure groups like Fathers4Justice has been in their ability to combine narratives of 'rights talk' with both 'welfare talk' and 'care talk'. And because this has occurred in the context of a proclaimed war against the unfair

---

12 Smart and Sevenhuijsen (1989).
13 DfES (2005).
14 Gillies (2005).
15 Bainham (2003a; 2003b); Collier (1995).
16 In *McKenzie*, the *National Newsletter of Families Need Fathers*, Issue 58, December 2003, the front page headline read 'Get political' and featured a message from Bob Geldof. The final paragraph read: 'This law can and will be changed. Use your agony and dismay. Channel it to action. Let every humiliation and tear move you forward so that no child nor man may suffer again what you have. Good luck!'
17 Geldof (2003).

privileging of mothers, the effect of their narrative has been an erasure of narratives of motherhood. Arguably, these movements have not been progressive, in the sense of trying to transform and share the responsibilities of parenthood (by, for example, campaigning for the right of fathers to work part-time); rather, they have been constructed in opposition to motherhood.

It is important, however, not to read every claim made by fathers in the field of family law as if it is merely the mouthing of a political doctrine fashioned by the fathers' rights movement. Equally, it is important not to assume that any father who becomes a party to an action in court is motivated by the same political goals. Yet there may be some evidence to suggest that the populist narrative of groups like Fathers4Justice is entering into everyday usage, and that it may be framing the claims made by more and more fathers. It is to these more complex issues that I shall now turn. First I shall examine a particularly significant case which articulates the new claims that fatherhood now makes in the field of family law. I shall then turn to some empirical examples of how fathers are expressing their contemporary engagement with (apparently privileged) motherhood and will look at how, in everyday constructions, the new narratives of fatherhood are taking shape.

The discursive (re)construction of fatherhood in family law

A significant case

The case I wish to consider in detail is *Re R (a child)*.[18] This was a case in which a man sought to claim parental responsibility in relation to a child who was not genetically related to him. In many ways, this case is the exact antithesis of 'old' paternity suits, in which mothers who had given birth to illegitimate children went to court to try to secure a ruling that a specific man was the biological father, in order that he could be required to pay maintenance.[19] In these cases, men were typically denying paternity and seeking to avoid a long-term responsibility for a child. In *Re R (a child)*, however, the man knew he was not the biological father, yet he was seeking to take on the responsibilities (which could include financial responsibilities) of a child, notwithstanding the fact that he was not in a relationship with the mother any longer.

The elements of this case as reported were that a child (a girl) was born in 2000 as a consequence of IVF treatment involving egg removal and embryo replacement, and anonymously donated sperm. The couple was not married, but had been in a long-term relationship and had been seeking assisted conception since 1994 as a consequence of the man's infertility arising from testicular cancer. The couple underwent one course of treatment, which did not result in pregnancy, but by the time the woman returned for the second and final course the couple had split up. She did not inform the clinic of this change in her circumstances. The

---

18 [2003] 2 All ER 131.
19 Marsden (1969).

second treatment was successful, resulting in the birth of a daughter who was the genetic child of the birth mother, but not genetically related to her former partner. On the birth of the child, the man (known as B) applied to the court for a parental responsibility order and a contact order. At this stage, the mother was in a new cohabiting relationship.

B was granted (indirect) contact and parental responsibility by the lower court. Hedley J stated: 'Accordingly I declare that pursuant to s 28(3) of the 1990 Act he is the legal father of this child.'[20] The judge's reasoning was straightforward. He argued that the couple entered into a joint enterprise together and neither of them withdrew consent to the treatment. Although their circumstances changed, the hospital was not informed, and so the original consent form was still the legitimate legal context which governed the birth of the child. Hedley J also pointed out that not only had the man agreed to be the legal father of a child who would not be genetically related to him, but a sperm donor had been selected whose general physical characteristics would match those of the prospective legal father.[21] Not surprisingly, much emphasis was placed on the meaning of the words in the 1990 Human Fertilisation and Embryology Act, and Hedley J's reading of this legislation meant that he concluded that a core purpose was for assisted reproduction to be facilitated in the context where a child would have a (legal) father. He felt therefore that there was a clear, simple and certain approach, namely one that recognised that there had been an original agreement from which neither had withdrawn, and the man was willing to be the father, and the 'provision' of a father was one of the desired goals of the Act.

In his judgment, Hedley J stated: 'Of course in this case one must have considerable sympathy with B. He wishes to be R's father and has responsibly fulfilled his obligations under my original order.'[22] This quotation is important because it reveals the influence of a man's claim that he 'wishes to be the father'. Perhaps because judges and others are so used to single men wishing to avoid being fathers, the mere assertion of the desire places the man in a very strong position. Of course, the 'wish' alone did not sway the case, but it is treated as central. This man fulfils the New Labour dream of the responsible parent who wants to embrace his duties, even though he is not actually a biological parent at all. In Hedley's judgment, the desirability for a child to have a father, as stated in the legislation on human embryology, was also an important factor. Basically, the legislation said that children need fathers, and here was a man who wanted to be a father.

The mother appealed against the judgment by Hedley J that her former partner should be granted a parental responsibility order (although she did not appeal against the indirect contact order), and the appeal was heard by Hale LJJ and others, with Hale providing the leading judgment. This time, the mother was

---

20 *B and D v R* [2002] 2 FLR 843, p 846.
21 Presumably this was important because it could be speculated that the child might resemble the non-genetic father's physical characteristics to some degree and that this strengthened his claim to becoming the legal father.
22 *B and D v R* [2002] 2 FLR 843, p 845.

successful and B was not granted parental responsibility. Hale argued (in agreement with the QC acting for CAFCASS) that

> ...s 28(3) is an unusual provision, conferring the relationship of parent and child on people who are related neither by blood nor by marriage. Conferring such relationships is a serious matter, involving as it does not only the relationship between father and child but also between the whole of the father's family and the child. The rule should only apply to those cases which clearly fall within the footprint of the statutory language.[23]

In this argument, Hale situated the parties in the context of their wider families. In other words, she did not just see it as a matter of simply establishing the man's relationship with the child, but she recognised all the other relationships which would be created by such a recognition of paternity. That is, she did not see this as an issue between two autonomous individuals, but as an issue of complex relationships involving several people. In this context, she went on to raise the question of whether the child would really benefit from the presence of her mother's former partner in her life. She notes that his presence in her life might actually harm the relationship between her mother and her new partner, so that the family in which she was being brought up might be destabilised. Finally, Hale returned to the issue of sympathy and whether it should guide legal judgment. She stated:

> ...it is helpful to consider whether the conclusion reached in a case where one's sympathies lie in one direction would be equally attractive in a case where one's sympathies would lie the other way ... Cases such as this, where a man wishes to assert paternity against a mother who wishes to deny it, are by no means uncommon. But had this mother been wishing to extract child support from this man, the court would have been slow to adopt a construction which would allow her to do so.[24]

Hale went on to argue that if the facts governing conception were unchanged, with the mother conceiving a child through some element of deception (as in this case), the courts would not have forced paternity onto the unsuspecting (genetically unrelated) former partner. Thus Hale proposed, by inference, that his claim to paternity should not be forced on the unwilling mother.

So, in the end, B was not declared to be the legal father of the child, but the final outcome is not necessarily the most significant issue here. This man can be seen to symbolise the new fatherhood. The fact of taking this case and arguing for a legal relationship to a child in circumstances which would have been virtually unimaginable even as recently as a decade ago provides a narrative form for the shape and substance of what good, dutiful fathers can now be like; moreover, the biological link is no longer seen as necessary to trigger this sense of responsibility. Hale located this case in the context of men's changing attitudes towards their responsibilities as fathers and pointed out that it was no longer unique that cases over paternity are now likely to be brought by men wanting to claim their legal status as fathers.[25] We cannot know, of course, whether more men want to be

---

23 *Re R (a child)* [2003] 2 All ER 131, p 137. See also Jones, Chapter 5 in this volume.
24 *Re R (a child)* [2003] 2 All ER 131, p 139.
25 See also Sheldon (2001).

recognised as fathers than before, but, if Hale is right, it may be that men are articulating this desire in new ways, namely through the courts and through avenues created by new interpretations of legislation. What is more, they are able to call upon the combined impact of 'rights talk', 'welfare talk' and 'care talk'. In this case, B deployed all three. His rights were generated by the original contract with the clinic; the 'welfare of the child' element was met by the provision of a father as required by the legislation; and care was evidenced by his willingness to take responsibility and to undertake actual care of the child. Hale's rejection of his arguments was based on a disagreement over whether the long-term welfare of the child would be met and also a reluctance to concede that the rights generated by the contract with the clinic could defeat the rights of the mother to resist his claim to have a legal relationship with her biological child. She also shifted the framework of his claim away from one which envisages an autonomous legal subject (namely the father) attempting to create a legal relationship with another legal subject (namely the child) to one in which all the parties are located in their wider families and webs of relationships. Hale therefore redefined fatherhood in terms of a set of relationships, rather than a narrow dyadic relationship between father and child. Her judgment can be seen as an alternative formulation of fatherhood, which rejects the new narrative of the father as a lone, heroic figure. However, it is not clear at this stage whether Hale's more relational vision of fatherhood or the more heroic version will gain ascendancy in family law.

Everyday narratives

Reading cases can provide only a partial insight into the scope of these new narratives of fatherhood; in particular, Appeal Court cases are not a window onto everyday life. Although such cases involve 'real' people, they become stylised and symbolic, and the arguments put forward for both sides are carefully manufactured and crafted. Cases, taken over time, can of course indicate how influential new forms of narratives are becoming, and individual cases such as *Re R (a child)* can indicate significant shifts in the sorts of claims that are being put forward as social and legal contexts change. But it is important to have some knowledge of how fathers speak in person, in more ordinary circumstances, about the claims they are making around fatherhood. So I shall turn to interview data with fathers[26] to explore the kinds of account they put forward. The excerpts selected here are from fathers who have been involved in disputes over contact or residence and, although their circumstances are not identical to those of the putative father in *Re R*, these interviews capture some of the same issues. They reflect the use of 'rights talk', 'welfare talk' and 'care talk', but also demonstrate a larger repertoire of accounts which break out of this formulation and perhaps reveal that, notwithstanding the emergence of newer narratives of fatherhood, more traditional forms

---

26 These excerpts are from interviews carried out in 2003–4 as part of a Department for Constitutional Affairs funded project on contact and residence disputes. For a full account of the study, see Smart and May (2005). We interviewed 27 fathers and 34 mothers in three different regions in England. All had been involved in disputes over contact or residence that had gone to court.

still exist. These excerpts also show the overlap between individual stories and the more political rhetoric of the fathers' rights movement.

Rights talk

In everyday narratives of fatherhood, 'rights talk' took the form of suggesting that, in law, fathers had fewer rights than mothers, and that fathers were treated as less competent and as having less of a claim to their children.

> Michael: Well I think, well it would be nice if you knew that there was no differentiation on sex; that father and mother would be treated exactly the same. I mean there is no doubt that at the moment it is expected that the mother will get residence. And I think these days a lot more fathers have a lot more input with the kids than they used to do. And to be excluded as a second class citizen I think is that is the one thing that I would like to see change.

This claim for equal rights was a recurrent theme in our interviews with fathers; we found that even where fathers were personally content with the outcome of their legal dispute, they nonetheless felt that other men were being discriminated against. Injustice and inequality may, therefore, be said to have become a strong inferential framework in everyday perceptions. In this context, a mother's argument that she may have been the primary carer throughout a marriage (giving up work, or working part-time) is seen as irrelevant to a claim which sees equality solely in terms of treatment meted out at the point of a court order. This claim for equality is therefore a completely decontextualised one, but it has a powerful resonance in a legal culture which is uncomfortable with claims about discrimination and unequal treatment. So, although 'rights talk' alone is insufficient to shift family policy away from the paramountcy principle and its focus on children's welfare, it does shift a generalised sense of 'sympathy' away from motherhood towards fatherhood.

Welfare talk

'Welfare talk' is typically based on the argument that it is always in the interests of children's welfare that they should have extensive contact with their fathers, even to the point of shared residence. As noted above, this is in line with government policy and also reflects the leanings of the courts and CAFCASS.[27] Unlike 'rights talk', it is also a narrative which is much used by mothers and by all the professionals involved in contact and residence issues. In a way, it has become almost a mantra.

> Nadeem: I don't see those children as a trophy. I don't see those children as a kind of bargaining chip if you like. I just want to do what is best for them.[28]

It is no longer clear how to read claims about welfare, since they can be harnessed to almost any style of parenting and any kind of arrangement. However, it is

---

27 Bailey-Harris (2001); Cantwell *et al* (1999).
28 Contact father, contact dispute.

equally true that parents are obliged to frame their disputes in terms of which parent has the welfare of the child most closely at heart. It is therefore little more than a rhetorical device; yet if it is absent, then parents are seen as making illegitimate claims.

Care talk

As I have suggested above, it is 'care talk' that can be particularly significant in the emergent narratives of fatherhood. In *Re R (a child)*, the putative father wanted to care and, although he had no experience of so doing, the desire to do so was seen as noble. In cases of divorce, the situation appears to be different, because the fathers have lived with their children and have had the opportunity to care – yet may not have actually done so. This means that, even in post-divorce situations, fathers are frequently voicing a desire to care in the future, rather than basing their claims on an existing care relationship.

> Stuart: At the beginning I don't think I was a good father; I think I did everything I was meant to do but I was just going through the motions. It was just as I got to know this little person, I grew to love him and it just doubles up and doubles up and then it gets out of control and you cannot control how you feel about him.[29]

Care talk is therefore often based on a rights claim: that is to say, many fathers are claiming a right to start caring or to care in the future. But the assertion of the desire to become a responsible, caring parent is treated as a natural urge that springs from instinctual love; it is therefore almost unassailable.

I have argued that the combination of rights, welfare and care talk combine to create a new narrative of fatherhood which is becoming influential in family law. It is, perhaps, important at this stage to restate that my focus is on accounts that fathers give and that seem to have particular salience for policy development. I am not suggesting that fathers use these arguments cynically (although obviously some may); rather I am interested in the degree of uniformity to be found across a very diverse range of fathers (of different ethnic backgrounds, from different social classes, and from different regions). It is as if, in finding a voice, fathers have all found the same one. This might suggest the power of the fathers' movement to provide a mode of articulation for the problems that fathers now face. Indeed, we might even find parallels between the way in which fathers have come to identify as a solidaristic, self-identified, 'minority' group and the impact on women of the rise of new feminist discourses in the 1970s and 1980s. Fathers – as a group – have been gradually politicised in Britain by the growth of women's rights in marriage and on divorce; by men's campaigns against the Child Support Agency; and more recently through fathers' claims to children. Moreover, for those fathers who go to court and who find that they do not get the orders they feel are justified, there is a sense of anger which is also unifying.

But it may be possible to over-emphasise the unity of this voice or narrative. On closer inspection, it is possible to see that fathers speak through a number of

---

29 Contact father.

different registers, emphasising different issues and emotions. By this, I mean that, although the main themes may appear to be similar (eg equal rights, welfare and care), we need to be attentive to how these are spoken, where emotional inflexions lie and the context in which such utterances are made. So, it is necessary to be attentive to other themes to see how fathers are presenting their 'story' and to understand how they wish to be perceived. Day Sclater has identified a number of narratives to be found when people tell the story of their divorce, the most common being the 'victim narrative' and the 'survivor narrative'.[30] We found evidence of similar ways of making sense of their experiences among the fathers we interviewed. But in addition we found some constructions which had strong overtones of the themes rehearsed in the fathers' movement literature. There is not space to consider all the variations here, but perhaps two of the most relevant are what might be referred to as the 'patriarchal narrative' and the 'heroic narrative'.

The patriarchal narrative

Richard: The simple truth was as the judge said in his own words 'It is normal for the children to live with their mother so that is where they will live.' Frankly I think that is a load of rubbish. It is not normal for the children to live with their mother. It is normal for the children to live with their father; that is the normal thing. The family follows the father. Where the father has work, the family goes with the father. That is normality. However, I lost the children who were forced to go back home.[31]

In this case, the father moved to work in another town and took his children with him, but he was made to return them to live with their mother. As he puts it, 'they were forced to go back'. Elsewhere in this father's account, he makes it clear that a mother who commits adultery should lose all her rights to the residence of the children. Not only did he argue that decisions should be made on the basis of matrimonial fault, but he argued that if they were, then women would not leave their marriages because they would not leave their children. In this account, there are very strong resonances of the debates on 'child custody' in the late nineteenth and early twentieth centuries, when it was argued that mothers should not be guardians of their legitimate children lest they felt able to leave their marriages.[32] Here it is possible to see that children are the lever that some men wish to utilise to keep women from straying. Although, in a parallel register, such fathers can claim that they have the welfare of their children at heart, the slippage into this patriarchal rhetoric suggests that welfare concerns may be secondary.

The heroic narrative

The heroic narrative has become particularly significant through the rhetoric of Bob Geldof;[33] it conjures up the image of the father taking on a hazardous battle against the odds in order to be able to play a part in his children's lives. Of course

---

30 Day Sclater (1999).
31 Contact father, residence dispute.
32 Brophy (1982).
33 Geldof (2003).